D0690596

"Information through Innovation"

Data Modeling

G. Lawrence Sanders

State University of New York – Buffalo

boyd & fraser publishing company

I(T)P An International Thomson Publishing Company

Danvers • Albany • Bonn • Boston • Cincinnati • Detroit • Madrid • Melbourne
Mexico City • New York • Paris • San Francisco • Singapore • Tokyo • Toronto • Washington

To mom, Phyllis, and dad, George

A volume in the boyd & fraser *Contemporary Issues in Information Systems* series.

Executive Editor: James H. Edwards
Editorial Assistant: Beth A. Sweet
Production Editor: Barbara Worth
Manufacturing Coordinator: Tracy Megison
Marketing Coordinator: Daphne J. Meyers

Production Services: Books By Design, Inc.
Composition: Gex, Inc.
Cover Design: Kevin Meyers
Cover Photo: Franklin Wagner, The Image Bank

bf ©1995 by boyd & fraser publishing company
A division of International Thomson Publishing Inc.

I(T)P The ITP™ logo is a trademark under license.

Printed in the United States of America

⊛ This book is printed on recycled acid-free paper that meets Environmental Protection Agency standards.

For more information, contact boyd & fraser publishing company:

boyd & fraser publishing company
One Corporate Place • Ferncroft Village
Danvers, Massachusetts 01923, USA

International Thomson Publishing Europe
Berkshire House 168-173
High Holborn
London, WCIV 7AA, England

Thomas Nelson Australia
102 Dodds Street
South Melbourne 3205
Victoria, Australia

Nelson Canada
1120 Birchmont Road
Scarborough, Ontario
Canada M1K 5G4

International Thomson Editores
Campos Eliseos 385, Piso 7
Col. Polanco
11560 Mexico D.F. Mexico

International Thomson Publishing GmbH
Königswinterer Strasse 418
53227 Bonn, Germany

International Thomson Publishing Asia
211 Henderson Road
#05-10 Henderson Building
Singapore 0315

International Thomson Publishing Japan
Hirakawacho Kyowa Building, 3F
2-2-1 Hirakawacho
Chiyoda-ku, Tokyo 102, Japan

7 8 9 10 MT 9

Library of Congress Cataloging-in-Publication Data

Sanders, G. Lawrence.
    Data modeling/G. Lawrence Sanders.
      p. cm.
    Includes index.
    ISBN 0-87709-066-1
    1. Database design. 2. Data structures (Computer science)
    I. Title.
QA76.9.D3S26 1995
005.74—dc20

94-37160
CIP

Contents

Preface

Two important circumstances led to the development of this book. The first involved teaching and consulting in the Peoples Republic of China in the late eighties and early nineties. China is an emerging economic giant with information processing needs that seem overwhelming. China needs computing technology, China needs data communications networks, China needs business education and training, and above all China needs time—time to develop a social environment that can accommodate this change.

The second circumstance that influenced the development of this book was a course that I have been teaching in the U.S. in systems analysis and design for over ten years. Students in groups of three identify an organization or department, analyze its operations from an information processing perspective, and design a system that will complement, enhance, or change the way data is processed.

Despite the many cultural, technological, and business differences between the two countries and their organizations, there is one dramatic similarity. Organizations in the U.S. and in China, to varying degrees, have a core data infrastructure that is inadequate. The data necessary to run the organization is not there, and if it is there, it is not readily accessible.

A great deal of database design work needs to be done out there. In my experience, data modeling with the entity relationship (ER) diagram is the best method for designing and redesigning databases, regardless of the database size.

BOOK HIGHLIGHTS

This book is about data modeling and ER diagrams. Chapter 1 discusses the role of data modeling in integrating organizational databases. Chapter 2 introduces the basic building blocks for constructing ER diagrams. An important feature of the ER modeling approach described in Chapter 2 is that it can be used to develop object-oriented data models and semantic-oriented data models for object-oriented databases and semantic databases.

Chapter 3 describes the *optional-max* approach for translating ER diagrams into relational tables. Typical approaches for translating ER diagrams into relational tables are difficult to apply because they involve many exception rules. The *optional-max* approach is straightforward and it produces tables where null values are minimized and the tables are in third normal form.

Chapter 4 presents a broad range of ER application areas, including production, accounting, human resources, customer support, customer tracking, and reservations systems. Chapter 4 is actually a catalog of ER models that can be used to initiate the data modeling process.

Chapter 5 presents data modeling from a strategic perspective. Enterprisewide data modeling, which attempts to identify strategic database opportunities, is a difficult, time-consuming process. The strategic data planning approach using a generic data model can be used to jump-start the enterprisewide data modeling process and make it more productive.

Chapter 6 illustrates that the most important activity of object-oriented analysis and design is constructing an object-oriented data model. The chapter also illustrates that the ER concepts described in this book have a direct correspondence with object-oriented data modeling approaches.

Relational table normalization is discussed in the appendix. Table normalization is a complementary topic to ER modeling and the appendix contains material on relational table normalization and the relationship between ER modeling and the normalization process.

INTENDED AUDIENCE

Over the years I have found my systems analysis and design students spending ever more time on database design and data modeling. This book is a direct result of that realization. For a variety of reasons, systems analysis and design books limit their coverage of data modeling. This book eliminates that deficiency.

Data Modeling can also be used as a supplemental text in database courses. Many database books limit their coverage of data modeling. This book will increase the student exposure to data modeling concepts. Students can use Chapter 4, which presents numerous examples of ER models, to understand and initiate the database design process.

This book can be particularly useful as a supplemental text in courses where students are learning to use some type of database management software, for example, SQL; client-server relational languages such as *Oracle, SQLWindows,* and *Power Builder;* or personal computer front-end relational languages such as *Microsoft Access, Paradox for Windows,* and *Dbase for Windows.*

The following sequence of learning activities works very well in courses where database management software is used. Students should first learn the basics of the language, including how to implement a relational join. Students should then learn the data modeling concepts outlined in this book. Students should then design, build, and implement a system from scratch. This final activity assists students in integrating the data modeling and relational language concepts.

Finally, the best way to learn how to use an automated design tool is to have some previous training and knowledge in the underlying modeling language. This is an opinion that has some empirical support in the research literature. *Data Modeling* can be used to gain the necessary background knowledge for applying computer-based ER modeling tools effectively.

ACKNOWLEDGMENTS

This book has benefited from the many outstanding individuals who have worked on data modeling. The references and the footnotes contained in this book present only a limited subset of these many people. I am, however, indebted to all.

I would like to thank Howard Foster, the interim Dean of the School of Management of the State University of New York at Buffalo, for giving me the opportunity to write the first draft of this book during sabbatical leave. I would also like to thank John Boot, the department chair, as well as the entire faculty in the Management Science and Systems department for their continuing support of this project.

My sincere gratitude to Valery Limpert and Ruth Sing for assisting me in typing, editing, and meeting deadlines. The graphics were particularly difficult and Valery assisted in designing the layout and preparing some of the more critical examples.

The following individuals helped shape this book with their invaluable feedback as reviewers of the manuscript in its various stages:

John Boggess	Purdue University
William Cornette	SW Missouri State University
Dick Howell	Lansing Community College
Elliott Kleinman	Miami Dade Community College
Bill Korn	University of Wisconsin–Eau Claire
Kuldeep Kumar	Georgia State University
David Paradice	Texas A&M University
Anne Rensel	Niagara University
Dave Russell	Western New England College
Joseph Sessum	Kennesaw State College
Laurette Simmons	Loyola College

A special thanks is extended to reviewers David Paradice of Texas A & M University and Kuldeep Kumar of Georgia State University. Their comments, insight, and willingness to discuss ideas at the most outrageous times were invaluable in completing this project.

It was a pleasure working with the team of professionals put together by boyd & fraser in support of this project. James Edwards, my acquisitions editor, orchestrated this team and was an unending source of confidence and encouragement. Daphne Meyers was very helpful in the early stages of this project, and Beth Sweet provided much guidance in completing the project and bringing closure. Barb Worth was invaluable in her often "behind the scenes" role of keeping everything moving in the right direction as quickly as possible without ever sacrificing quality. Elizabeth MacDonell and Nancy Benjamin provided valuable editorial assistance that improved both the content and presentation of the material. I greatly appreciate their efforts on my behalf.

The students in my systems analysis and design course deserve special recognition. They used this manuscript in its various early manifestations and some of their systems analysis and design projects are used as examples herein.

Finally, I would like to thank my family for their patience and support. In particular, a heartfelt thanks to Jody and Sean for creating the climate that made this book possible.

Data
Modeling

1 Database Design and Systems Integration

Key Concepts

systems integration
data modeling
entity relationship (ER) diagram
database design
logical schema
data repository
normalization
physical schema

Increased global competition and markets, the geographic scattering of corporate functions, and increased sensitivity to customer demands for new products and services are putting tremendous pressure on organizations and their infrastructures for transmitting and processing information. As organizations age, they often engage in activities that are now unnecessary or perhaps even detrimental to the current organizational mission even though they were appropriate when first instituted. Systems integration is one response used by users and management to streamline, recast, and—most important—recapture the organization by restructuring their information systems architecture (see Highlight 1.1).

In this chapter, we discuss the role of systems integration and database design in revitalizing an organization's information restructuring efforts. After a brief look at the definition and goals of systems integration, we review the history of database design and then outline its three phases. Finally, we discuss the benefits of strategic data modeling and systems integration in an organization.

Highlight 1.1 Systems Integration Strategies and Definitions

The term *systems integration* as used here is an umbrella term denoting the various activities involved in restructuring the information systems architecture. Although systems integrators and consultants use various strategies to integrate the organizational information systems infrastructure, they all use some form of systems analysis to accomplish their goals. These strategies are briefly defined here.

Reengineering

Reengineering is the process of analyzing, modeling, and modifying an existing organizational system so that the system is supportive of organizational processes in delivering quality products and services. One of the key activities in reengineering is looking for ways to streamline how information is processed. The root of many systems integration problems lies in an organization's complex tapestry of software and data with a legacy that can be traced to the first manila folders and file cabinets. Systems that are built on old business principles are called legacy systems. Some organizations thrive and others wither on their legacy systems.

Downsizing

Downsizing, sometimes called rightsizing, usually involves scaling back the hardware platform. Endusers often complain that their localized processing and decision-making needs are not being met by the centralized information systems department, and downsizing has been promoted as a way to reduce costs, speed applications development, and put computing power in the hands of the endusers. In a typical scenario, the organization migrates from a centralized mainframe to a microcomputer-based LAN architecture. The resultant microcomputer

(continued on next page)

configuration is often called a client–server architecture. For many businesses, the client–server approach involves a variety of personal computers and mainframes with integrated connectivity. With the client–server network configuration, a micro, mini, or mainframe computer (called the server) has special resources, such as an abundance of disk space or a high-speed laser printer, or specialized software that client computers can utilize. For example, a client computer can send a message to the server computer requesting customer data. The server or file server can then retrieve the appropriate customer information from the database and send it back to the client's application.

Outsourcing

Outsourcing is the contracting of various systems functions, such as data entry, programming, facilities management, disaster recovery, and telecommunications management, to outside providers of services. The primary reason that organizations turn to outsourcing is cost reduction. However, organizations also use outsourcing as a means to increase their adaptability to changes in the marketplace. For example, they may acquire access to technical expertise that is not available internally. Outsourcing has some risks, including an insecure work force and the potential to lose control of the function being outsourced, both of which could result in lower-quality products and services.

Total Quality Management

Total quality management (TQM) is a philosophy wherein the process for conceptualizing, producing, and delivering products is constantly being improved to meet consumer demands. TQM as applied to information systems means the process for conceptualizing and producing an information system is constantly being improved and the information systems product itself is constantly being improved to meet customer demands. The TQM approach mandates cooperation and participation by management and employees to deliver customer-oriented products and services.

Systems Integration and Databases

Database integration is the process of identifying organizational data requirements, formalizing data requirements with a conceptual model, and instituting structure and control on the data model and on data access to ensure database integrity and stability. Systems integration typically centers on so-called common databases, which are used by several organizational departments and functions. Examples might include customer, order, human resources, and inventory databases. Systems integration often involves the merging of diverse hardware, software, and communications systems into a new consolidated operating unit.

Information Engineering and Strategic Data Planning

These are approaches to systems integration in which database requirements are linked to information systems planning and organizational strategy. The construction of an enterprisewide data model is an important activity in these approaches.

Systems integration is often defined as the merging of diverse hardware, software, and communications systems into a new consolidated operating unit. This is a narrow view of systems integration that slights the importance of database design. The philosophy espoused in this book focuses on the importance of database design in systems integration. In this context, **systems integration** is a two-phase iterative cycle that includes:

1. The process of identifying and formalizing data requirements with a conceptual data model—using a graphical language to represent data.

2. The implementation of the conceptual data model in the appropriate hardware and software configuration.

The process of modeling and formalizing data requirements with a conceptual modeling tool, called **data modeling**, is an intrinsic part of the database design process. The primary tool used in conceptual data modeling—and the focus of this book—is the **entity relationship (ER) diagram.**

Systems integration has several goals, such as to transform an existing system into a more efficient system and, more important, to develop a system that is more supportive of organizational processes, thereby making the organization both more efficient and more competitive. Typical systems integration strategies involve new hardware and software platforms, the restructuring of applications programs, the development of new telecommunications networks, and complete system rewrites.

The primary objectives of database design are to provide flexible, timely, and secure access to the right data so as to enhance organizational productivity.

Not too long ago, organizations had a difficult time integrating the various subsystems because information technology was expensive, and there were limited conceptual tools for guiding and modeling organizations. Now, however, we are in an era where telecommunications networks and relational databases are cost effective. What's more, advances in hardware and software technology, database design, and strategic management are providing the foundation for integrating organizational systems. Many of the classic examples of strategic information systems described in Figure 1.1, for example, are built on large integrated databases. On-line reservation systems, order entry systems, and customer support systems use wide-band transmission lines, high-performance hardware, and sophisticated interface technologies to communicate with these databases. These systems have resulted in greater operational efficiency and more differentiated products and services.

- American Hospital Supply's order-entry distribution system is built around the firm's product or catalog database and its customer order database. This system permits customers to peruse the product database, then enter orders for necessary supplies through the customer order database.

- Merrill Lynch developed the cash management account (CMA) system around customer and customer account databases for checking, credit card, and brokerage services. The CMA system required a complex interface between the Merrill Lynch brokerage databases and Banc Ones check and credit card databases.

- McKesson has tied its purchasing system into the order entry systems of its 40 largest suppliers so that replenishment orders can be entered directly. McKesson was able to reduce the number of distribution centers from 85 to 55, and the number of buyers from 120 to 14. Nevertheless, the buyers now handle twice the volume of the old system.

- American Airlines' and United Airlines' Sabre and Apollo systems are actually built upon the flight databases and customer databases. The complexity and scope of these two systems have preempted market entry and have also permitted United and American to offer new services.

- Sears, Roebuck and Company maintains the largest customer database in the United States, with 40 million entries. Sears uses this database to target special consumer segments, track purchasing activity, and interest stores. The database also helps Sears integrate and provide information to its various subsidiaries such as Allstate Insurance, Dean Witter Reynolds brokerage, and Coldwell-Banker real estate brokers.

FIGURE 1.1   Examples of Strategic Information Systems Built on Database Access*

*cf. Cerveny, Pegels, and Sanders, 1993.

On the other hand, databases that have not been adequately integrated exhibit several symptoms that reduce the ability of organizations to function effectively, as illustrated in Figure 1.2.

What are the symptoms of a lack of integration, particularly of poorly integrated databases? If a company answers yes to any of the following questions, it is likely that there are problems with the level of database integration.

- We cannot retrieve data from organizational databases. We know that the data exists in the computer, but it cannot be combined or retrieved in a suitable manner without significant effort from our systems people.

- Management reports are provided one or two weeks after end-of-month, quarter, or yearly closing.

- Employees are engaging in lots of intermediate data reentry, summarizing, reorganizing, and recalculation before reports are issued.

- Some departments and employees have difficulty obtaining data in a desired format.

(continued on next page)

- Some departments and employees cannot do their job effectively because the data is simply not available anywhere.
- Some departments are doing things with their data that are making it hard for other departments to do their job effectively.
- Sometimes customers receive two bills, we lose track of what we have in inventory, and we lose track of our customers or vendors. Employees, customers, and vendors sometimes receive letters at the wrong address.
- We do not know where a product is in the production process, our equipment is improperly maintained because we do not know what equipment has or has not been maintained, and we have trouble matching employees to jobs.
- End users from functional areas (marketing, finance, production, and so on) are always complaining about their inability to obtain data.

FIGURE 1.2   The Organizational Integration Index

THE EVOLUTION OF DATABASE DESIGN

Systems analysis, database design, and information systems planning were once considered separate activities. Database design was treated as a separate topic and offered as a separate course from systems analysis and design. Now, however, database design is viewed as an intrinsic part of the entire development process, and textbooks on systems analysis and design cover data modeling and normalization.

Ideas from corporate strategy are also being integrated into database design. The practice of aligning the information systems planning process with the corporate planning process has come not only at the prompting of information systems professionals but also from senior-level executives who recognize that it makes sense to analyze and plan for the implementation of any technology that organizations have and will continue to invest in so heavily. Information technology can improve organizational efficiency; more importantly, it can provide organizations with a competitive edge.

The integration of strategy with database design and systems analysis and design has been labeled *information engineering* and *strategic data planning*. An initial activity in the information engineering and strategic data planning processes is the construction of a macro-level data model or enterprisewide data model. In Chapter 5, we present a strategic data planning approach for developing an enterprisewide data model. An example of a more detailed systems development life cycle that incorporates strategy as well as database design concepts can be found in Figure 1.3.

Strategic Information Systems Planning
- Evaluate current strategic position
- Determine future strategic emphasis
- Align information systems planning with organization strategic plan
- Construct enterprisewide data model
- Construct high-level process model
- Assess areas for technological improvement and exploitation

Systems Analysis
- Analyze user data requirements
- Refine and expand enterprisewide data model to incorporate logical views
- Begin constructing data repository
- Model processes using data flow diagrams (DFDs)
- Integrate data and process models

Systems Design
- Input form design
- Design reports
- Design screens
- Select DBMS implementation: hierarchical, network, relational, and so on
- Design database repository
- Plan for implementation and training

Detailed Systems Design
- Select storage media
- Determine access methods
- Design procedures and tasks
- Design programs
- Configure hardware
- Configure data communications network

Systems Implementation
- Code programs
- Test programs and overall system architecture
- Install system

Systems Maintenance and Support
- Correct errors in analyis, design, and programming
- Enhance system to reflect new requirements
- Audit system on an ongoing basis to ensure that it reflects organizational needs

FIGURE 1.3 **Contemporary Systems Development Approach**

A number of automated tools for downstream development activities (for example, automated program code generators) can be used to support the actual implementation of the system. In contrast, the tools for automating systems analysis and conceptual and logical data modeling are rather modest, consisting primarily of drawing tools, normalization algorithms, and computerized data dictionaries and data repositories. Tools are also available that take existing organizational files and reverse-engineer data in those files to create a conceptual data model. This technology is somewhat immature at present, and it may never reach its purported potential. Consider the following argument by Batini, Ceri, and Navathe [1992, p. 11]:

> First, we should emphasize that conceptual design cannot be very much helped by automatic tools; the designer has full responsibility for the process of understanding and transforming requirements into conceptual schema. After the first conceptualization, many database systems offer tools for fast prototyping, using fourth generation languages for application generation, screen, and report formatting. These tools may be directly available to the nonprofessional for developing simple databases, and they ease the work of professional database developers. Thus, we believe that conceptual design is by far the most critical phase of database design, and further development of database technology is not likely to change that situation.

Conceptual modeling is indeed a difficult task. This book will present the ER diagram as an important tool for constructing a conceptual model. But it will present more than just the features of this modeling language; it will also provide directions, guidelines, and examples that will assist the data modeler in constructing conceptual data models.

Database design, which is concerned with identifying and implementing a database structure, along with systems analysis and design, are simply problem-solving strategies for constructing systems [Cerveny, Garrity, and Sanders, 1990]. The problem, which can also be viewed as an opportunity, is the perceived gap between the current state of the data in the database and its desired state in the system. Reducing the difference in the gap requires an analysis of the existing database structure. Through a recursive analytical process, alternative database structures are identified and redefined. Finally, in the last phase of the problem-solving process, a particular data architecture is selected and implemented.

Systems development modeling tools, such as data flow diagrams, screen painters, prototypes, and ER diagrams, support the problem-solving process in two ways. First, modeling tools help in problem decomposition and problem structuring. Second, they are used as communication tools between user and analyst, between analysts, and even between users. Analysts perceive the world differently from the user community, and as Figure 1.4 illustrates, communication and communication tools often help reconcile different world views. The reconciliation of the user's view of the world with the analyst's view of the world is an important element in developing systems that satisfy the user's needs and the information needs of the entire organization.

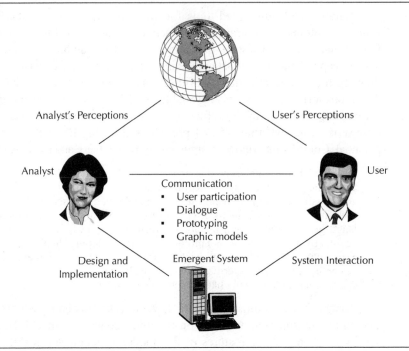

FIGURE 1.4   Communication Assists in Reconciling World Views

PHASES OF DATABASE DESIGN

As Figure 1.5 shows, the database design process attempts to answer the following questions: What data is important? How will the data be represented? Where will the data be stored? It is important to note the distinction between systems analysis and design and database design. In database design, much more so than in systems analysis, the focus is on developing a comprehensive organizational database to support organizational tasks. Systems analysis, on the other hand, considers database requirements, but it also considers data flows, data transformations, input and output design, and procedures for processing data.

A typical implementation of the database design process includes the following phases: conceptual database design, logical database design, and physical database design.

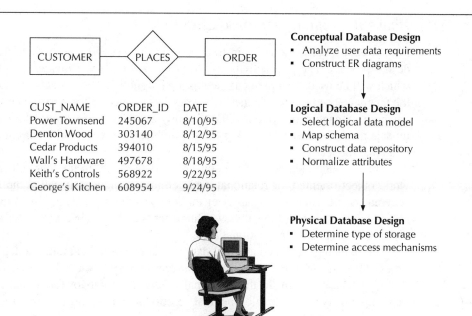

Conceptual Database Design
- Analyze user data requirements
- Construct ER diagrams

Logical Database Design
- Select logical data model
- Map schema
- Construct data repository
- Normalize attributes

Physical Database Design
- Determine type of storage
- Determine access mechanisms

CUST_NAME	ORDER_ID	DATE
Power Townsend	245067	8/10/95
Denton Wood	303140	8/12/95
Cedar Products	394010	8/15/95
Wall's Hardware	497678	8/18/95
Keith's Controls	568922	9/22/95
George's Kitchen	608954	9/24/95

FIGURE 1.5 **The Database Design Process**

Phase I: Conceptual Database Design

Conceptual database design revolves around discovering and analyzing organizational and user data requirements. This includes identifying what data is important and what data should be maintained. The major activity of this phase is identifying entities, attributes, and their relationships, and constructing ER diagrams to represent them. The ER diagram is used to specify what data is important to the organization and to the various database users. When the data modeling process encompasses the entire organization, it is called the *corporate data model* or the *enterprisewide data model*.

Formalizing organizational data requirements with conceptual models serves two important functions. First, conceptual models help users and systems developers identify data requirements. Conceptual models are by design abstract. As such, they encourage high-level problem structuring and help establish a common ground on which users and developers can communicate to one another about systems functions. Second, conceptual models are useful in understanding how existing systems can be modified. Typically, even the most simple standalone system can be better explained and represented with an abstract model.

Phase II: Logical Database Design

Formal data specifications begin to emerge in this second phase of the database design process. The first activity in this phase is to select a *logical data model*, which will be used to implement the conceptual model. The logical data model is the language used to specify the logical database structure for a particular type of database management system (DBMS) software. There are several logical data models to choose from, including the hierarchical, network, object-oriented, and relational models.

The resultant encoding of the conceptual data model in the hierarchical, network, object-oriented, or relational data definition language is called the **logical schema**. A subschema is a subset of the logical schema. This is also sometimes referred to as a view or logical view. Thus, there can be a subschema or view for a division, department, or functional area.

The mapping of the conceptual data model to the logical data model, sometimes called *schema mapping* or *schema conversion*, is the primary activity of logical database design. In the relational model, the focus of this book, schema mapping involves the development of relational tables and the assignment of attributes to the tables.

Another important function of the logical modeling phase is the construction of the **data repository**, which is sometimes referred to as the data dictionary or project dictionary. The data repository is essentially a catalog of all the data items and their characteristics, including their format and how they are related to other data items. It describes each entity, attribute, and relationship in terms of its purpose, ownership, name, format (character, numeric, date, and so on), domain (valid characters and valid numeric ranges), and access restrictions. The enforcement of data repository standards through naming and format conventions is necessary to maintain database stability and integrity. It is not uncommon to find that various organizational constituencies have different names and maintain redundant data for customers, employees, and inventory.

Another important activity in the logical database design is **normalization**, which is a process for assigning attributes to relational tables that reduces data redundancy, eliminates data anomalies, and provides a robust data architecture for retrieving and modifying data. It is thus a complementary process to ER modeling that further enhances the long-term integrity of the database. As an interesting aside, ER modeling simplifies the normalization process. Correctly constructed ER diagrams and similar types of conceptual models produce naturally normalized relational schemas [Hull and King, 1990; Schmid and Swenson, 1975]. We discuss normalization in the Appendix for those readers wanting more detail on the topic.

Phase III: Physical Database Design

The third phase of the database design process involves actually deciding how the logical model and data repository description can be represented in computer hardware, that is, where and how entities, attributes, and relationships will be stored and accessed. The description of how data is physically stored in the computer is called the **physical schema**. Decisions made at this stage include the type of storage media used, where records are stored on the media, the access methods used to retrieve data (sequential, direct, indexes, and lists), and how to fine-tune the system to achieve maximum systems performance.

As database technology has increased in sophistication, there has been a change of emphasis on the phases of database design, which has relegated physical database design to a smaller role. In hierarchical database management systems environments, the database administrator spends more time on designing and implementing the physical schema. Examples of physical schema design in a hierarchical DBMS environment include deciding the actual physical placement of data on disk, determining what data records to index, and dealing with various optimization issues so as to increase database access performance.

A logical data model is supposed to be independent of its physical implementation on a media. In reality, the implementation of hierarchical data models in hierarchical database management systems is commonly linked to the hardware it will be installed on. However, with the emergence of relational database management systems, the emphasis has been moved upstream toward logical and conceptual database design. Thus, in an organization that uses a relational database management system, the database administrator spends more time working with organizational constituencies to identify what data elements should be maintained in the database and to understand the logical relationships that exist among the various data elements. With relational database management systems, many of the physical database design issues are handled by the relational DBMS software.

THE BENEFITS OF DATA MODELING

Data modeling, when incorporated into the strategic data planning and enterprisewide data modeling processes, provides a strong foundation for integrating organizational databases. When data modeling involves senior-level managers, it forces them to look toward operations for strategic opportunities. It also cultivates a strategic perspective in managers because it forces them to look at the data relationships throughout the firm and to understand how systems are interdependent. Broad-based participation in strategic enterprisewide integration is necessary for identifying areas in which an organization needs to capture data as well as for identifying outdated, irrelevant systems.

Organizations can take steps to improve their level of integration by simply recognizing that basic transaction databases are the foundation and future of strategic information systems. Organizations have now entered a phase where databases are being used strategically, to solve problems, and to realize new business opportunities.

Strategic enterprisewide systems integration is not a large-versus-small organization issue. For a large organization, the cost of integration and the subsequent conversion of existing systems can be in the millions of dollars. However, the benefits of integration—knowledge and efficiency—provide a strategic synergistic edge. If integration takes place in a planned, modular, and consistent fashion, enhancements and modifications to the system will be simplified. This is particularly important in the development of strategic partnerships because the success or failure of a merger or acquisition can hinge on the degree to which their respective systems are compatible.

Further, organizations can realize the benefits of data modeling without developing a full-blown enterprisewide data model. A subset data model, developed for a department or a business activity, can provide the foundation for systems integration. A subset ER diagram is a local optimum because it has been normalized and can therefore be readily combined with other ER models to develop a global data model.

Small companies can derive equal if not greater benefits from systems integration and data modeling than larger companies. Small companies usually do not have numerous functional area databases with their complex interdependencies, and they have not reached the point where the organization is so complex that the users and system developers cannot comprehend its dimensions and details. Small organizations can be integrated and migrated to a new database platform that supports flexible data access and simplifies database integrity and stability within a manageable period.

SUMMARY

This chapter served as an introduction to systems integration and its goals and benefits to an organization attempting to restructure its information transmitting and processing. We looked briefly at the evolution of database design as the basis for systems integration and at the three phases involved in the database design process. Finally, we considered some of the benefits an organization—large or small—may reap when it incorporates systems integration into its strategic planning. In the next chapter, we begin to look more closely at the data modeling concepts, including the semantic model, ER diagramming, attributes, and entities.

Review Questions

1. What are the various strategies an organization can use to restructure its information systems infrastructure?

2. What are the benefits of systems integration to the organization?

3. Why is data modeling an integral part of the database design process?

4. Suppose you are implementing a database design for a midsized manufacturing company. What are the basic steps you would take to enact the design? Would you follow the same process for a smaller or larger company? Why or why not?

2 Introduction to Data Modeling Concepts

Key Concepts

entity relationship (ER) method
entities
attributes
relationships
entity occurrence
semantic network concept
aggregation abstraction (Is-part-of)
generalization and specialization abstraction (Isa)
association abstraction (Is-associated-with)
composite attributes
simple (atomic) attributes
multivalued attributes
cardinality
recursive relationships

The **entity relationship (ER) method** is a popular data modeling approach to database design that was first published by Peter Chen in 1976. The ER approach is a high-level data modeling language—often called an abstraction tool—that can be used to understand and simplify the world of data relationships and complex systems. The ER modeling approach discussed in this chapter integrates the powerful concepts of semantic modeling and object-oriented modeling. Semantic modeling, of which ER modeling is a type, has been used by linguists to represent the meaning of words and by researchers in artificial intelligence as a mechanism for knowledge representation. In this chapter, we discuss the three basic data representation types and symbols used in ER diagramming. We follow this with a discussion of how the semantic network primitives can be used to conceptualize and complement the ER model. Finally, we discuss how cardinality relationships between entities are determined by organizational business rules.

ER DIAGRAMMING: TERMINOLOGY AND CONCEPTS

An ER diagram uses three basic graphic symbols to conceptually represent organizational data (see Figure 2.1). **Entities**, which are conceptual data units or data objects, are represented with rectangles. **Attributes**, which describe the characteristics or properties of entities, are represented as circles. **Relationships**, which depict the structural association that exists between entities, are represented with diamonds. Although any graphic symbol can be used to represent the semantic

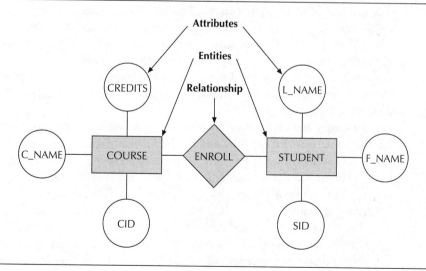

FIGURE 2.1   ER Attribute Diagram

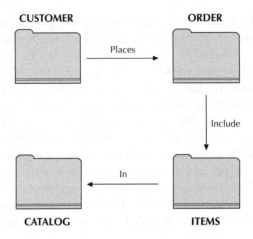

CUSTOMER   ORDER

Places

Include

In

CATALOG   ITEMS

FIGURE 2.2   **ER Diagrams Can Be Constructed with Different Graphic Symbols When Presented to Users**

data structures, as long as the symbols are used consistently (Figure 2.2), in this book we use the popular symbols mentioned. Many of the software packages for data modeling do not include the circle symbol for attributes on the ER diagram, but instead permit the user of the software instant access to the attribute characteristics through the data repository.

ENTITIES

The concept of an entity is central to understanding data modeling and relational databases.[1] Organizations capture and maintain data about people, transactions, assets, things, and even concepts. The things about which organizations keep data are called entities. Another way to conceptualize an entity is as a class of objects. Objects are things in the real world that can be observed and classified because they have related properties. The terms *class* and *entity* are in effect identical and can be used interchangeably.

An **entity occurrence** or an instance of an entity, is the result of an entity having some or all its values assigned to the attributes. An entity instance is essentially a data object. Put simply, there is some person, place, or thing that exists. This is similar to the tuple concept in relational databases or the record concept in traditional file processing. In Figure 2.3, for example, Jim Kelly and his related attributes form an instance of the entity EMPLOYEE. Or put another way, Jim Kelly and his related attributes are an object of the class EMPLOYEE.

Entities can be tangible, such as a person, building, materials, or tools. They can also be intangible, such as in the case of an employee benefit plan, a sale, or a

---

[1] Some authors use the term *entity type* to denote classes of objects.

EMPLOYEE Entity	**Values**
Conceptual Attributes	
■ SOCIAL_SEC_NUM	517494930
■ LAST_NAME	Kelly
■ FIRST_NAME	Jim
■ POLITICAL_AFFILIATION	Democrat
■ HEALTH_PLAN	HMO
Physical Attributes	
■ HEIGHT	6.3′
■ HAIR	Brown
■ WEIGHT	220
■ SEX	Male
■ AGE	32
Spacial Attributes	
■ ADDRESS	Null
Structural Attributes	
■ MANAGED_BY	Levy
■ MANAGES	Offense

INVENTORY Entity	**Values**
Conceptual Attributes	
■ WHEEL_ID	A-6052
■ DESCRIPTION	Bicycle wheel
■ REORDER_POINT	500
Physical Attributes	
■ DIAMETER	27″
■ WIDTH	1 1/4″
Spatial Attributes	
■ LOCATION	Warehouse B
Structural Attributes	
■ ASSEMBLY_SEQUENCE	Follows frame
■ PART_OF	Frame

FIGURE 2.3   Potential Attributes for EMPLOYEE and INVENTORY Entities

political party. Many times intangible entities have tangible representations. For example, a stock certificate represents the abstract concept of corporate ownership, the possession of certain intangible skills and intellectual ability are represented by a tangible certificate of graduation, and a sales receipt is a tangible object that represents a sale. A useful way to think of an entity is that it is a conceptual unit that is described by attributes.

How do you identify entities? In general, entities are identified and defined by the organization and its users. There is no all-encompassing catalog or list of every possible entity. (We present a modest catalog of ER diagrams in Chapter 4.) To be sure, there are standard or generic entities that have evolved across many organizations—for example, customers, employees, and product entities. But many entities evolve with an organization and are specific to the particular way an organization conducts its business.

THE BASIC STRUCTURAL MODELS OF ENTITIES AND ATTRIBUTES

The **semantic network concept**, also referred to as an associative network concept, was developed by Quillian [1968] as a way to model human memory and represent the meaning of words. The essence of this approach is that the meaning of a word—its semantics—can be determined by its relationship to other words. The semantic network concepts are simple but very powerful; they have been used by artificial intelligence researchers to model knowledge, by computer scientists to develop object-oriented languages, and by database researchers to model databases and construct database management software. In Chapter 6, we use the principles of semantic networks to illustrate object-oriented data modeling.

Three structural primitives are the basis of semantic network modeling. The *Is-part-of* primitive is used to model how something can be constructed from components, the *Isa* primitive is used to model inheritance, and the *Is-associated-with* primitive is used to model interaction between entities. To explain these concepts further, consider the following types of relationships that can exist between entities and attributes:

1. An entity can be constructed, described, and qualified by its attributes and by other entities (the *Is-part-of* structure). In essence, the entity is constructed from components consisting of attributes and other entities. This is referred to as the **aggregation abstraction**.

2. An entity can be related to other entities through entity subclasses (the *Isa* structure). An entity subclass inherits attributes from the entity superclass and has its own unique attributes. This is referred to as the **generalization and specialization abstraction**.

3. An entity can interact with other entities and can affect the attribute values of other entities (the *Is-associated-with* structure). This is referred to as the **association abstraction**.

The *Is-part-of*, *Isa*, and *Is-associated-with* structures are all part of semantic modeling and can be used to conceptualize and implement an ER model. Figure 2.4 is an example of a typical semantic network model, and Figure 2.5 is the ER diagram translation for the semantic model. A more detailed description of how the aggregation, generalization and specialization, and association abstractions can be used to construct ER diagrams follows.

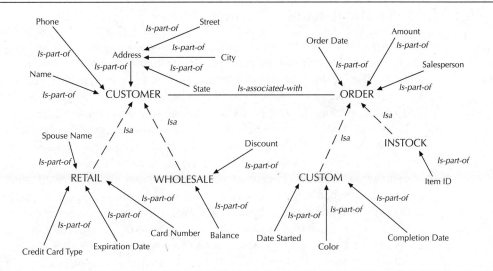

FIGURE 2.4   Semantic Data Model

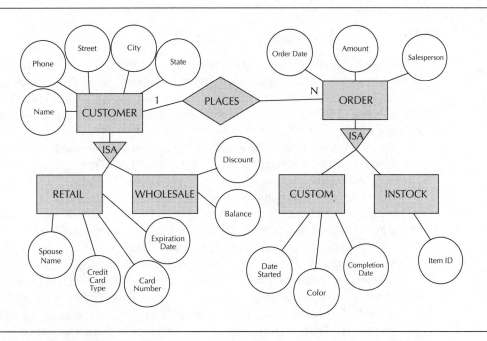

FIGURE 2.5   Semantic Model Converted to ER Diagram

An attribute is essentially an elementary component or property of an entity. An entity can be characterized as being an aggregation of attributes (see Figures 2.4 and 2.5). The *Is-part-of* aggregation structure is used to conceptualize this structure. For example, Name *Is-part-of* CUSTOMER, Address *Is-part-of* CUSTOMER, and Phone number *Is-part-of* CUSTOMER; similarly, Order Date *Is-part-of* ORDER, Amount *Is-part-of* ORDER, and Salesperson *Is-part-of* ORDER.

Words used to describe the *Is-part-of* structure include *has, contains, consists-of, embodies, incorporates, encompasses, holds, comprised-of, embraces, piece-of, element-of, member-of, segment-of, component-of,* and *includes*. As illustrated by Figure 2.3, another way to think of attributes is how they delineate or qualify an entity in terms of the entity's physical, structural, spatial, and conceptual dimensions.

In most ER modeling implementations, the *Is-part-of* relationship between an entity and an attribute is represented by a line connecting the entity graphic—the rectangle—to the attribute graphic—the circle. In many computerized implementations of ER modeling, attributes are not even shown on the ER diagram. They are, however, linked to the appropriate entity and are readily retrievable from the data repository.

Composite Attributes

A **composite attribute**, sometimes called a group attribute, is an attribute that is formed by combining, or aggregating, related attributes. Several composite attributes are represented in the semantic diagram shown in Figure 2.4 and in the ER diagram shown in Figure 2.5, including Name, Address, and all the attributes that describe a Date.

The Address attribute, as illustrated in Figure 2.6a, has been defined in terms of the **simple** or **atomic attributes** Street, City, and State. These are called simple attributes because they are not divisible into any simpler data unit.

The customer Name is also a composite attribute, but the customer's first name and last name, which are simple attributes, are not shown on the semantic diagram in Figure 2.4 or the ER diagram in Figure 2.5. Similarly, all the attributes that represent a Date (Order Date, Date Started, Expiration Date, and so on) are composite attributes consisting of the simple attributes year, month, and day.

A composite attribute can be represented on an ER diagram by linking the simple attributes to the composite attributes, such as those shown in Figure 2.6b.

When an ER diagram is initially constructed by the database designer, some of the attributes are depicted on the diagram as composite attributes (for example, name and address). With subsequent refinement of the ER diagram, and the conversion

a. Semantic Model

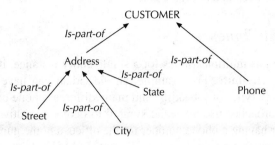

b. ER Model Showing Composite Attribute and Multivalued Attribute

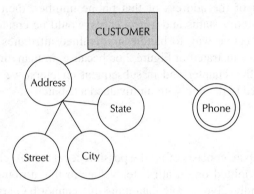

c. ER Model Showing Simple Attributes for Address and New Entity Phone

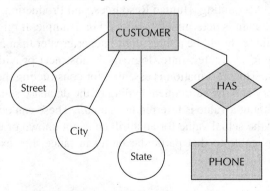

FIGURE 2.6   Composite and Multivalued Attributes

to relational tables imminent, the composite attributes are replaced with simple or atomic attributes, as illustrated in Figure 2.6c.[2]

Multivalued Attributes

When an attribute has multiple values for a single entity instance, it is referred to as a **multivalued attribute**. For example, an individual can have many educational degrees, many types of job skills, and many different phone numbers. Some data modeling approaches use a special symbol to depict a multivalued attribute such as a customer having a phone number for the office, a home number, a cellular number, and an emergency number (see Figure 2.6b). Each of these numbers could be represented as a simple attribute (Office#, Home#, Cellular#, Emergency#). But if more information was needed, such as who was to be contacted at that number or the address of that phone number, then the attribute would be elevated to entity status and a new entity would be created for it. The simplest and most effective way to handle multivalued attributes is to elevate them to entity status as illustrated in Figure 2.6c because, in many instances, they *are* entities. Later in this chapter and in subsequent chapters, we present additional discussion related to dealing with multivalued attributes.

Attribute Domain

The *domain* of an attribute consists of all the possible legal values, categories, and operations that are permitted on an attribute. Values in the attribute domain are drawn from a set of indivisible atomic data units that cannot be parsed or further divided into meaningful units. For example, the domain for weight is drawn from the set of valid values for weight. The domain for department might consist of the categories Finance, Accounting, Human Resources, and Production.

The attribute domain is determined by users. For example, it might be decided that the weight attribute should be a three-digit integer greater than 50. The format or data type (integer, character, date, logical, or abstract) provides additional domain information. This information is essential for constructing the data dictionary or data repository and the subsequent coding of the database schema.

An attribute without a value is referred to as a *null*. These can occur for one of two reasons: Either the actual value for an attribute is not known or the attribute in question is not applicable to that particular entity instance. For example, notice

---

[2] Only simple or atomic attributes are permitted in typical relational databases. All composite attributes must be converted to atomic attributes when defining a relational table.

that in Figure 2.2, Jim Kelly's value for address is null because it is not known. One of the important goals of relational database design is to minimize the occurrence of null values in the database.

ENTITIES AND THE Is-part-of *AGGREGATION STRUCTURE*

Entities can also be combined to form an aggregate entity. The *Is-part-of* structure is also used to describe the aggregation of entities. Remember that the *Is-part-of* structure between entities is represented as a relationship on the ER diagram using the diamond graphic symbol.

Consider the following example of aggregation. A computer can be viewed as an aggregation of several components that are each entities unto themselves. Thus, in Figure 2.7, MOTHERBOARD *Is-part-of* COMPUTER, HARD DRIVE *Is-part-of* COMPUTER, and MONITOR *Is-part-of* COMPUTER. Notice, however, that the *Is-part-of* label has been replaced with *has*, *contains*, and *consists-of*. These labels are then used along with the diamond graphic on the ER diagram to denote the *Is-part-of* relationship. In other words, although the *Is-part-of* relationship exists in fact, in practice, synonyms are used to model the aggregation structure. These synonyms include *has, contains, consists-of, embodies, incorporates, encompasses, holds, comprised-of, embraces, piece-of, element-of, member-of, segment-of, component-of, encompass,* and *includes*.

As another example, consider that a division within an organization can be an aggregation of several departments (see Figure 2.8). Thus, the accounting department *Is-part-of* division, the human resources department *Is-part-of* division, the production department *Is-part-of* division, and the marketing department *Is-part-of* division.

ENTITIES AND THE Isa *GENERALIZATION–SPECIALIZATION STRUCTURE*

Entities can also have *subtypes* or *subclasses* and *supertypes* or *superclasses*. The relationship between an entity subtype and its parent is referred to as an *Isa* relationship. The *Isa* structure is used to model the relationship between entities, where one entity is a generalization of several more specialized entities, and is represented on the ER diagram as an upside-down triangle (see Figure 2.9). Note that in some data modeling implementations, it also may be represented by a diamond with the *Isa* label placed inside.

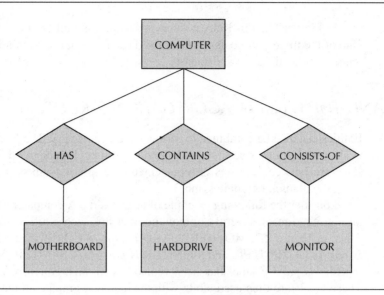

FIGURE 2.7   Component Entities Aggregated to Create a Computer Entity

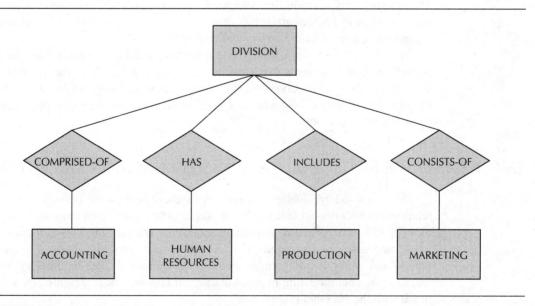

FIGURE 2.8   Department Entities Aggregated to Create a Division Entity

The idea behind the *Isa* structure is that some entities are subsets of a more general entity. The supertype entity is said to be a *generalization* of the subtype *specialization* entities. Each subtype entity inherits attributes from the supertype entity. But each supertype entity also has unique attributes of its own.

For example, as Figure 2.9 illustrates, the entity supertype or superclass for STUDENT could consist of the attributes Student_Id, Name, Address, Sex, and Age. Entity subtypes for STUDENT might include GRADUATE and UNDER-GRADUATE students. Thus GRADUATE *Isa* subclass of STUDENT, and UNDERGRADUATE *Isa* subclass of STUDENT as well. These subclasses would inherit all the attributes for STUDENT—Name, Address, and so forth—but each would also have additional unique attributes. Graduate students might have additional attributes indicating whether they passed their qualifying exams or completed their thesis requirement. In contrast, undergraduate students might have additional attributes for extracurricular activities in social fraternities and

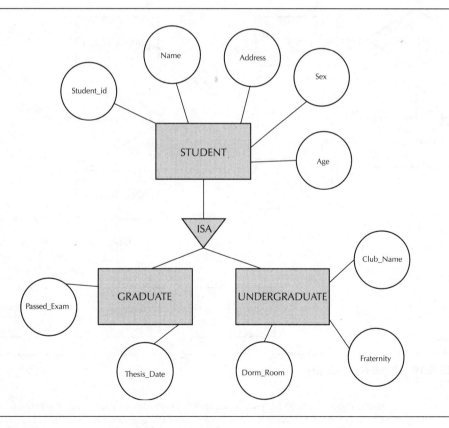

FIGURE 2.9 An *Isa* Structure for Students

clubs. Furthermore, the supertype entity STUDENT is referred to as a generalization of the GRADUATE and UNDERGRADUATE entities, whereas the subtype GRADUATE and UNDERGRADUATE entities are described as specializations of the STUDENT entity.

In another example, shown in Figure 2.10, suppose a bank offers commercial loans or home equity loans. In this case, LOAN would be the entity supertype, and HOME_EQUITY loan and COMMERCIAL loan would be the entity subtypes. LOAN would be a generalization entity, and HOME_EQUITY and COMMERCIAL would be specializations of LOAN. In object-oriented terms, LOAN would be the superclass, and HOME_EQUITY and COMMERCIAL would be subclasses.

Figure 2.10 also illustrates how the *Isa* structure is used to model the different types of collateral for commercial loans.[3] Commercial loans can be secured with stocks, property, and insurance. There are certain attributes that these collateral

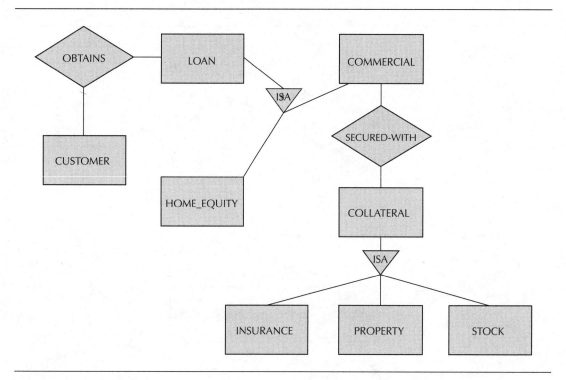

FIGURE 2.10   Bank *Isa* Structure

[3] Home equity loans are typically secured with the home itself, and the attributes maintained are simply the address and the equity position of the homeowner.

types have in common. For example, general class attributes for collateral might include the manager who presided over the gathering of the documentation for the collateral, the date the documentation for the collateral was presented, and the total value of the collateral. However, each type of collateral also has unique attributes. In the case of the PROPERTY subclass, there would be attributes for its location and the name of the primary lienholder. Likewise, unique attributes for the INSURANCE subclass might include the policy number, face value of the policy, and the type of policy. Finally, attributes for the STOCK subclass might include the stock description, the stock name, the number of shares, and the value of the shares. Like LOAN in the previous example, here COLLATERAL is the generalization entity, and INSURANCE, PROPERTY, and STOCK are specialization entities.

ENTITIES AND THE Is-associated-with STRUCTURE

There are instances when two entities have very few attributes in common but may nonetheless engage in transactions with each other. These transactions can be modeled with an ER diagram using the *association abstraction*. As an example, consider an employee who is assigned a company automobile. An employee entity has very few attributes in common with an automobile entity; however, when an employee is assigned an automobile to be used in the execution of his or her job, the organization records the transaction and attempts to maintain information on who has been assigned to a particular car. The relationship between employees and cars is shown in Figure 2.11. The employee-assigned car structure is represented on the ER diagram as a diamond. The ASSIGNED label along with the diamond graphic is used to denote the *Is-associated-with* structure.

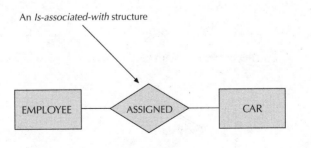

FIGURE 2.11 Relationship Is an *Is-associated-with* Structure

The *Is-associated-with* structure is used to model relationships where entities participate in activity that causes attribute values to change. The relationship itself does not represent dynamic activity, per se, but it does provide evidence that entities have engaged in transactions with other entities and that attribute values have been modified. As with the *Is-part-of* primitive, the *Is-associated-with* label is not used directly on ER diagrams. Instead, it is replaced by verbs such as *obtain, place, order, diagnose, use, request, register, initialize, assigned, give, take, create, distribute, move, drive, fly, rent, buy,* and *update*. For example, CUSTOMER *PLACES* ORDER (Figure 2.5) or CUSTOMER *OBTAINS* LOAN (Figure 2.10).

The *Is-associated-with* relationship can also be viewed as an aggregation of two entities. In Figure 2.12, for instance, the CUSTOMER entity and the ORDER entity can be combined to form the CUST_ORDER relationship. Similarly, the CUSTOMER entity and the LOAN entity can be aggregated to form the CUST_LOAN relationship. Some data modelers always try to use a verb to represent the relationship between entities, and others prefer the aggregation approach where entity names are combined. In many cases, an appropriate verb cannot be found to describe a relationship, and combining the names of the two entities is the only practical solution.

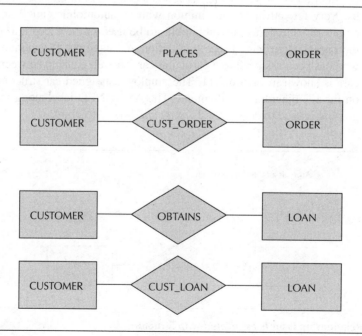

FIGURE 2.12   Relationships Can Be Labeled Using Verbs or Aggregate Names

Updating is the most common *Is-associated-with* relationship. Indeed, the major work effort in most applications is directed toward file or table updating. The initiation of an order by a customer activates algorithms for updating entity instances in the CUSTOMER entity (for example, customer balance) and the ORDER entity (for example, adding a new order with the appropriate customer and product information). Again, the interaction between two entities is manifested by changes in attribute values in the two entities or the addition and deletion of new entity instances.

It should also be noted that some data modeling approaches do not make any distinction between entities and relationships. You and your organization may also choose to represent some relationships as entities. Although this book is definitely partial toward using the relationship structure to model data, good results can be obtained from a variety of data modeling approaches. What is important is the ultimate goal, which is to translate the ER diagram to third-normal form relational tables. We discuss relational table normalization in the Appendix for those desiring further background on the topic.

ELEVATING ATTRIBUTES TO ENTITIES

Attributes commonly evolve into entity status as they become more important to an organization. Although it is not always easy to determine whether an attribute should be treated as an entity, two key indicators may help you in deciding.

The first indicator that an attribute should be considered an entity is that the attribute has *related important attributes*. For example, suppose that a student record has information on the student's hometown. If the hometown name is the only attribute of interest, then Hometown is simply an attribute of the student record. If, however, the school administration decides to maintain demographic information, such as the population and primary industry on each hometown, then Hometown could be elevated to entity status.

As another example, in some organizations a job skill might be simply an attribute of an employee, whereas in others employee skills are corporate resources, and each skill may have a variety of detailed attributes associated with it. In this latter case, job skills would probably be considered an entity rather than an attribute. As another example, color might simply be an attribute for describing your own bicycle. To a paint company, however, color would very likely be an entity with attributes consisting of the types of dyes and the amount of dye necessary to produce the color. In sum, if the data item in question has a unique identity and it has attributes, then it should probably be an entity.

The second indicator that an attribute should be an entity is that the attribute is *multivalued*. Recall that multivalued attributes have multiple values for a simple entity instance. There are many approaches to modeling multivalued attributes, but the simplest and most efficient way to handle multivalued attributes is to elevate them to entities if at all possible.

It is much easier to model the complexity of a multivalued attribute and to subsequently convert an ER diagram to relational tables when multivalued attributes are treated as entities. Multivalued attributes are always more complex than they first appear. For example, consider the job skills of an employee or the phone numbers for an employee. They typically have unpredictable ranges of occurrences (the number of skills possessed by each employee), and they usually have related attributes (skill category, detailed skill description, and so on) that are of interest to the organization.

CARDINALITY

The relationship between two entities can also be described in terms of the **cardinality**, a numerical mapping between entity instances. In the simplest sense, cardinality is the maximum number of records in one file that are linked to a single record in another file and vice versa. Cardinality can be expressed as one-to-one (1:1), one-to-many (1:N), or many-to-many (N:M). The N and M terms indicate that the cardinality is greater than one.

The cardinality of a relationship depends on a particular organization and its business rules. These business rules are typically identified by interviewing users and examining the current system and its accompanying documentation. For example, in some organizations it is a business rule that customers can have more than one outstanding order (1:N), whereas in others it is a business rule that a customer can have only one outstanding order (1:1).

Figure 2.13 presents a simple example of a 1:1 relationship where an organization has the following business rules related to employee car assignments:

Each employee is assigned to only one car.

Each car is assigned to only one employee.

Situations where the cardinality is 1:N (one-to-many) or N:M (many-to-many) relationships are more complex. Figure 2.14 presents an example of a 1:N cardinality relationship where a video rental store has the following rules:

Each customer may rent as many videos as desired.

A video can be rented by only one customer.

The cardinality mapping—or the degree of the cardinality—between CUSTOMER and VIDEO in this situation is one-to-many (1:N).

Figure 2.15 illustrates a situation where there is a one-to-many relationship and a many-to-many relationship. In the first example in Figure 2.15, a particular

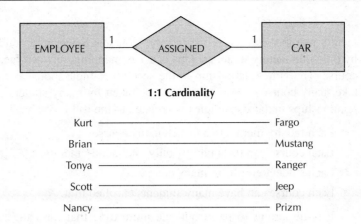

1:1 Cardinality

Kurt ——————————— Fargo
Brian ——————————— Mustang
Tonya ——————————— Ranger
Scott ——————————— Jeep
Nancy ——————————— Prizm

FIGURE 2.13   One-to-One Cardinality

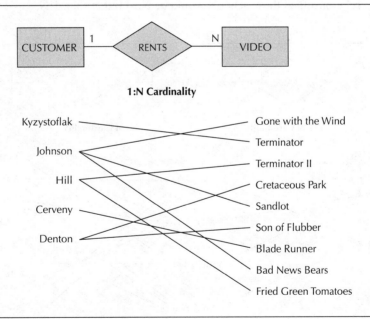

1:N Cardinality

Kyzystoflak ——————————— Gone with the Wind
Johnson ——————————— Terminator
Hill ——————————— Terminator II
Cerveny ——————————— Cretaceous Park
Denton ——————————— Sandlot
Son of Flubber
Blade Runner
Bad News Bears
Fried Green Tomatoes

FIGURE 2.14   One-to-Many Cardinality

faculty member can teach one or more courses; however, a course can be taught by only one faculty member. This is a 1:N mapping between faculty member and course. The N:M relationship in the second example indicates that a student can take many courses and a course can be taken by many students. The cardinality relationships in these examples are related to the following business rules:

Each faculty member can teach many courses.

Each course can be taught by only one faculty member.

Each student enrolls in many courses.

Each course can have many students enrolled in it.

It is important to point out one more time that the cardinality mapping is related to organizational business rules because they may differ from one organization to another. For example, at some colleges, there is a business rule that a course can have more than one faculty member assigned to it, thus the teaching relationship at these schools would be N:M rather than 1:N.

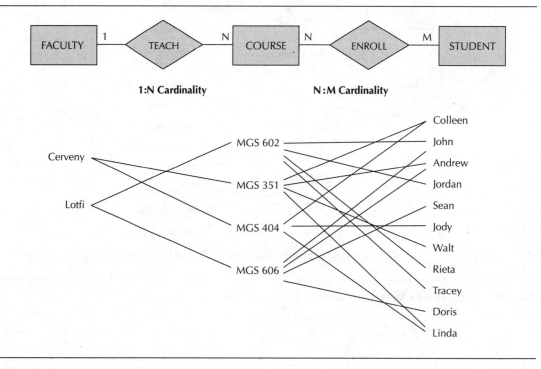

FIGURE 2.15   **One-to-Many and Many-to-Many Cardinality**

RECURSIVE RELATIONSHIPS

When an entity participates in a relationship with itself, the relationship is said to be **recursive**. Suppose an organization has an EMPLOYEE entity and wants to keep track of employees who are married to each other using this entity. This is a 1:1 recursive relationship that involves the EMPLOYEE entity. Figure 2.16 illustrates how this type of relationship is modeled with an ER diagram. As you can see, an entity participating in a recursive relationship is connected to itself. Thus Mike is married to Barb, Rieta is married to Walt, and so on. The bill-of-materials and the parts explosion relationships are classical examples of recursive relationships where the entity *Is-part-of* itself. In Chapter 3 we demonstrate how recursive relationships are modeled and subsequently converted to relational tables.

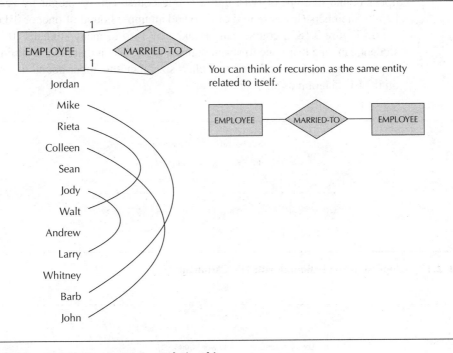

FIGURE 2.16   One-to-One Recursive Relationship

All the examples in the previous section described the cardinality relationship between two entities in terms of an *upper bound* or *maximum cardinality*. Recall that cardinality is the maximum number of records in one file that are linked to a simple record in another file and vice versa. The cardinality mapping between two entities also has a lower bound, which provides even more information about the relationship between entities. In the simplest terms, the *lower bound* for cardinality is the minimum number of records in one file connected to a single record in another file and vice versa. Several examples will illustrate how upper and lower cardinality bounds are represented on an ER diagram.

First, the diagram in Figure 2.17 has the following interpretation: A single faculty member can teach from zero to four courses (lower bound of zero and an upper bound of four, or 0:4), and a single course can be taught by zero or one faculty members (lower bound of zero and an upper bound of one, or 0:1).

In Figure 2.18, a course can be taken by zero to many students (0:N), and a student can take from one to seven courses (1:7). When there is uncertainty on the upper bound, such as in the case of class size, then the upper bound is represented on the ER diagram as an N or M.

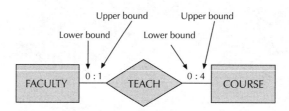

FIGURE 2.17   Upper and Lower Bound with 1:N Cardinality

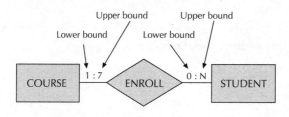

FIGURE 2.18   Upper and Lower Bounds with N:M Cardinality

When the lower bound for cardinality is zero, the relationship is referred to as *optional*. When the lower bound for cardinality is one, the relationship is called *mandatory*.

Referring to Figure 2.18, it follows that the relationship from COURSE to STUDENT is *optional* because the lower bound is zero and the relationship from STUDENT to COURSE is *mandatory* because its lower bound is one. Consider the *optional* case first. In this example, there is a business rule from COURSE to STUDENT that during a semester a course can enroll from zero (lower bound) to many students (upper bound). The cardinality mapping from COURSE to STUDENT is therefore *optional* because a course does not have to have any students enrolled in it. In other words, a given course, say Introduction to Data Modeling, could be part of the school curriculum and in the course catalog, but the course may not be offered every semester. Thus, Introduction to Data Modeling can be in the COURSE file, and there may be from 0 to 50 student records associated with the course in a given semester. Again, the lower bound of zero indicates participation in the relationship is *optional*.

Refer again to Figure 2.18 in considering the *mandatory* case. There is a business rule from STUDENT to COURSE that during a semester a student can take a minimum of one course (the lower bound) to a maximum of seven courses (the upper bound). The cardinality mapping from STUDENT to COURSE is defined as *mandatory* because most schools require that an individual, to be considered an active student and have an active student record, be enrolled in at least one course. In other words, if there is a record in the STUDENT file for Sean O'Casey and his related attributes, for example, then there must be at least one record in the COURSE file linked to Mr. O'Casey. In most colleges and universities, there is such a business rule, and this business rule affects the way in which the database is designed and ultimately implemented.

Now refer to Figure 2.17. The relationship between FACULTY and COURSE and the relationship between COURSE and FACULTY are both *optional*. In this example, there is a business rule from FACULTY to COURSE that during a semester a faculty member can teach from zero courses (the lower bound) to a maximum of four courses (the upper bound). The relationship from FACULTY to COURSE is thus optional. Faculty members on sabbatical or sick leave do not teach courses during the semester, but they still maintain faculty status.

Similarly, the cardinality mapping from COURSE to FACULTY is also optional. That is, a course does not have to have a faculty member assigned to it (the lower bound of zero), or it can have one faculty member assigned to it (the upper bound of one). Thus a course can be in the catalog, but it might be offered only once every two years, and when it is offered, it is taught by only one faculty member.

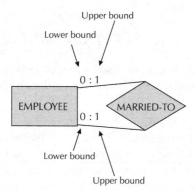

FIGURE 2.19   Upper and Lower Bounds for 1:1 Recursive Relationship

Finally, recursive relationships can also have upper and lower bounds. The recursive relationship in Figure 2.19 has the following interpretation: An employee can be married to zero or one employees. This ER diagram reflects that some employees will be married to one another. In effect, there is a two-way optional relationship from EMPLOYEE to EMPLOYEE because employees do not have to be married to one another.

It is not uncommon in the early stages of database design to exclude the lower bounds for the cardinality mapping; however, the lower bounds are important when the ER diagram is finally used to define the tables for the relational database system. In the next chapter, we illustrate how both the upper and lower bounds for cardinality determine what relational tables will need to be created in order to reflect organizational business rules.

SUMMARY

ER modeling is a very powerful tool for simplifying the representation and conceptualization of complex systems. It is not only useful for complex integrated applications; even modest-sized standalone systems are difficult to comprehend without the aid of a powerful abstraction tool such as the ER diagram.

In this chapter, we discussed how the semantic modeling structures of aggregation (*Is-part-of*), generalization and specialization (*Isa*), and *Is-associated-with* can be used to conceptualize data and assist in the construction of ER diagrams. We also discussed how organizational business rules are used to model the cardinality relationship between entities. In the next chapter, we will demonstrate how the concepts outlined in this chapter can be used to define the tables in a relational database.

Review Questions

1. Describe the three basic data representation types used in ER diagramming. What are their symbols? What are their functions? How are they identified? Give examples of each.

2. Briefly define each of the three structural primitives used in ER modeling. What are their functions? How are they identified? Give examples of each.

3. When might an attribute be elevated to entity status?

4. What are the cardinality relationships for the following rules?

   • Each department can have only one manager.

   • Each manager can work in only one department.

   • Each department can have many employees.

   • Each employee can work in only one department.

5. Are the cardinality rules stated in question 4 optional or mandatory? Why?

3 Converting ER Diagrams to Relational Tables

Key Concepts

primary key
schema mapping
optional-max conversion
foreign key
intersection table
concatenated key
binary relationship
ternary relationship
n-ary relationship

Recall that an entity relationship diagram is a highly abstract conceptual representation of organizational data. The relational model, the focus of this chapter, is also a type of conceptual model, but it is a more restrictive, lower-level conceptual model that requires all data be placed in tables or relations. Although there is a degree of correspondence between how data is represented in an ER model and in the relational model, the translation is not perfect. For instance, whereas the relational data model uses identifiers—called **primary keys**—to link knowledge in one relation to knowledge in another table, a primary key is not required in an ER diagram (though they are often included). The ER diagram uses the lines between entities to depict knowledge relationships, and the relational model uses primary keys to represent relationships.

An attractive feature of the ER diagram is that it is independent of the details of implementation. This is true whether we are talking about a relational, hierarchical, network, or even an object-oriented database.

The method used to convert the conceptual data model representation, in this case the ER diagram, into relational tables is sometimes referred to as **schema mapping** or schema transformation. The goal of this chapter is to illustrate how an ER diagram can be used to define and create a relational schema for a relational database management system. Specifically, we discuss using the *optional-max* conversion process for transforming an ER diagram into relational tables as it applies to each type of cardinality relationship—1:1, 1:N, N:M. We also discuss the conversion process for *Isa*, aggregate, and recursive relationships. Finally, we introduce the concept of *ternary* relationships and present some issues of performance versus flexibility in database design. Definitions related to relational databases and ER modeling that are relevant to this discussion are presented in Figure 3.1.

It is important to remember that an ER model can also be used to create schema definitions for object-oriented, hierarchical, and network databases as well as be used to identify the files for a file-oriented programming language such as BASIC, C++, or COBOL.[1]

BASIC CONVERSION RULES

Three simple rules are the basis for converting an ER diagram into relational tables. These rules, which follow, use cardinality information (see Chapter 2) to determine what relational tables are needed to reflect the organizational data requirements:

[1] For an overview of how to convert ER diagrams into hierarchical and network databases schema, see Gillenson [1987], Howe [1989], and Batini, Ceri, and Navathe [1992]. For a discussion of the relationship between ER models and object data models, see Rumbaugh et al. [1991] and Palmer [1994].

Entity:	Any tangible or intangible object about which data is stored.
Relation or table:	A two-dimensional table that is the implementation of data about entities in the relational model. The columns are the attribute names. The rows are entity instances or tuples. It is similar to the file concept.
Attribute:	A characteristic, quality, or property of an entity. A column in a relational table. A field in a record.
Entity or object instance:	A tuple or row in a relational database. It is similar to a record in a file.
Domain:	The domain of an attribute consists of all the possible legal values, categories, and operations that are permitted on an attribute. If an attribute does not have a value or the value cannot be applied, it is referred to as a NULL.
Candidate key:	An attribute or set of attributes that uniquely identifies each row, tuple, or entity or object instance in a table.
Primary key or identifier:	An attribute or combination of several attributes that is selected from the set of candidate keys to uniquely identify each row, tuple, or entity or object instance in a table.
Concatenated or composite key:	A primary key consisting of two or more attributes that uniquely identify each row, tuple, or entity or object instance in a relational table.
Foreign key:	This is an attribute in a relational table that is not by itself the primary key of the table, but it is a primary key in another table. Foreign keys are used to join attributes in tables and implement organizational business rules in relational databases.

FIGURE 3.1   **Important Definitions for Converting ER Diagrams to Relational Schema**

- For 1:1 cardinality relationships, all the attributes are merged into a single table.
- For 1:N cardinality relationships, post the identifier from the "one" side as an attribute to the "many" side.
- For N:M cardinality relationships, create a new table and post the primary keys from each entity as attributes in the new table.

These rules will in many instances result in acceptable relational table definitions. However, they will not guarantee that null attribute values are minimized. Recall that an attribute without a value is called a null. If there is one topic that many of the database theorists agree on, it is that null-valued attributes should be avoided [cf. Codd and Date, 1993].

When null values for attributes are permitted in a relational database, it is difficult to construct and interpret relational database queries [McGovern, 1994]. The *optional-max* approach that we detail in the next section guarantees that the relational tables will have the minimum number of null values.

THE Optional-Max *CONVERSION PROCESS*

As we noted, the cardinality relationship between two entities (1:1, 1:N, or N:M) is used to convert the ER diagram to relational tables. It is the *upper* bound for cardinality that determines what relational tables will be created. However, it is the *lower* bound that determines if the upper bound should be treated as a "many." In other words, a relationship that appears to be 1:1 may be better represented as a 1:N relationship, and one that appears to be 1:N may be better represented as an N:M relationship when defining the relational tables. This is the case when the lower cardinality bounds are *optional*—that is, zero—and the upper cardinality bounds are one.

The *optional-max* approach treats an entity with an optional lower bound as if it had a "many" upper bounds. By temporarily labeling the upper bounds as "many," you guarantee that the relational tables you create will have the minimal number of nulls.

Optional-Max *Conversion*[2]

Following are the rules for converting an ER diagram into relational tables using the *optional-max* approach:

1. Construct an ER diagram, and label the upper and lower bounds for cardinality. All multivalued attributes should be represented as an entity.

2. In every instance where the lower bound for cardinality is 0 and the upper bound is 1, temporarily label the upper bound as N. If the upper bound is greater than 1 (for example, 3 or 10 or N), leave it as is.

3. Use the entity name for each entity as the table name.

---

[2] The approach outlined here, called the *optional-max* method, avoids the numerous exception rules and cases that are given by many data modelers for handling *optional* relationships. Another benefit of the approach is that it does not require a shift in terms of how cardinality is represented on ER diagrams such as in the case of the min-card and max-card labeling described by Batini, Ceri, and Navathe [1992]. For additional discussion on how *optional* relationships are handled using special cases and exceptions, see the discussion by Batini, Ceri, and Navathe [1992] on partial participation relationships, the discussion by Howe [1989], and the discussion by Bruce [1992] on independent and dependent entities.

4. If an identifier or primary key has not been selected, then select an identifier for each table.

5. Take all the attributes that describe an entity and post them as column names in the relational tables.

   Note: Rules 6, 7, and 8 relate only to the upper cardinality bounds. All upper bounds greater than 1 should be treated as a "many."

6. For 1:1 relationships, merge all the attributes into a single table. The name for the relational table can be one of the entity names that participate in the 1:1 relationship, a composite name formed by combining the two entity names, or a new name that reflects the meaning of the data in the table.

7. For 1:N relationships, take the identifier of the "one" side of the 1:N relationship and post it as an attribute to the "many" side. The identifier posted to the "many" side is a **foreign key**.

8. For N:M relationships, create a new table and use the relationship name as the name for the table. The resulting new table is called an **intersection table**. The identifier for the intersection table is a **concatenated key** that is created by posting the primary keys from the two entities that participate in the relationship. Each identifier posted to the new intersection table is a foreign key.

9. Take any additional attributes that describe entities or relationships and post these as column names in the appropriate relational table. If there are any composite attributes in the relational table definition, decompose them into simple or atomic attributes.

Figure 3.2 presents a simplified ER diagram of a hypothetical school. Note that all the *optional* relationships that have an upper bound of 1 (cardinality is 0:1) are relabeled with an *N* on the ER diagram. The *optional-max* rules are then used to convert the ER diagram in Figure 3.2 to the following relational tables.

The following relational tables are the result of converting the ER diagram in Figure 3.2. The primary keys or identifiers for each table are underlined, and the foreign keys are in italics. A few representative attributes have also been included in the table definitions.

FACULTY	(<u>FID</u>, F_NAME, L_NAME)
TEACH	(*<u>FID</u>*, *<u>CID</u>*)
COURSE	(<u>CID</u>, C_NAME, CREDITS)
ENROLL	(<u>CID</u>, *<u>SID</u>*, GRADE, CREDITS)
STUDENT	(<u>SID</u>, *MAJ_ID*, F_NAME, L_NAME, H_STREET, H_CITY, H_STATE)

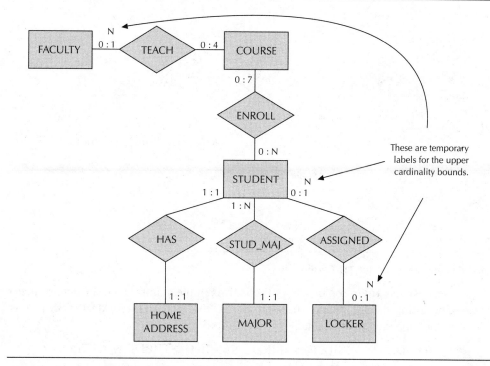

FIGURE 3.2   **ER Diagram to Be Transformed into Relational Tables Using *Optional-Max* Approach**

MAJOR   (MAJ_ID, DESCRIPTION)

ASSIGNED   (SID, *LID, BUILDING*)

LOCKER   (LID, BUILDING)

Let's examine in greater detail how these relational tables were constructed using the *optional-max* approach.

One-to-One Upper Cardinality Bound

The only relationship in the ER diagram in Figure 3.2 that exhibits one-to-one cardinality (1:1) is the relationship between STUDENT and HOME_ADDRESS. The business rules for this particular relationship are:

A student has one and only one home address.

A home address has one and only one student.

In this example, the various attributes for the home address (H_STREET, H_CITY, H_STATE) are simply posted to the STUDENT table, as shown in Figure 3.3. (Although two students could conceivably reside at one home address,

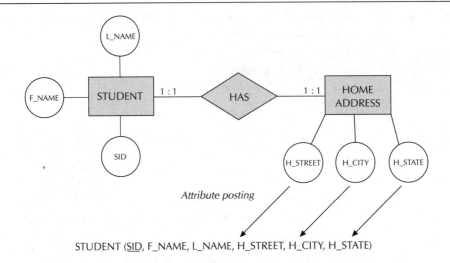

STUDENT (<u>SID</u>, F_NAME, L_NAME, H_STREET, H_CITY, H_STATE)

FIGURE 3.3   **Posting Attributes for 1:1 Cardinality**

the business rules for this hypothetical example ignore such an occurrence.) Converting the 1:1 relation between STUDENT and HOME_ADDRESS results in the following relational table:

STUDENT   (<u>SID</u>, F_NAME, L_NAME, H_STREET, H_CITY, H_STATE)

One-to-Many Upper Cardinality Bound

The relationship between STUDENT and MAJOR represents the only true one-to-many (1:N) relationship in the ER diagram in Figure 3.2. For purposes of this example, a student at this institution is allowed only one major. In some schools, the business rule is that a student can have more than one major. The business rules for these two entities are:

A student has one and only one major.

A major has one to many students.

Converting the 1:N relationship between MAJOR and STUDENT, using rule 7 of the *optional-max* approach, is illustrated in Figure 3.4. The conversion results in the following relational tables:

STUDENT   (<u>SID</u>, *MAJ_ID*, F_NAME, L_NAME, H_STREET, H_CITY, H_STATE)

MAJOR   (<u>MAJ_ID</u>, DESCRIPTION)

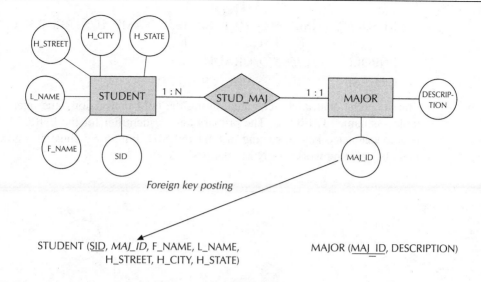

STUDENT (SID, MAJ_ID, F_NAME, L_NAME,
H_STREET, H_CITY, H_STATE)   MAJOR (MAJ_ID, DESCRIPTION)

FIGURE 3.4   **Posting Foreign Keys with 1:N Cardinality**

In essence, MAJ_ID, which is the primary key for the MAJOR relational table, is also a foreign key in the STUDENT table. Thus MAJ_ID links the MAJOR table and the STUDENT tables. If the major—and hence the MAJ_ID—is known, then all the students who have that particular major can also be located. Figure 3.4 also illustrates how primary key posting works for 1:N relationships.

Many-to-Many Upper Cardinality Bound

Several relationships in Figure 3.2 use the many-to-many rule (see rule 8) to convert the ER diagram to relational tables. For N:M relationships, a new table is created. The primary keys from the two entities that participate in the relationship are then posted to the new table. For example, the relationship between COURSE and STUDENT is N:M. The business rules for these two entities are:

A student must enroll in one to seven courses.

A course can enroll zero to many students.

Converting the N:M relationship between STUDENT and COURSE results in the following relational tables:

STUDENT   (<u>SID</u>, *MAJ_ID*, F_NAME, L_NAME, H_STREET, H_CITY,
           H_STATE)

ENROLL   (<u>*CID*</u>, <u>*SID*</u>, GRADE)

COURSE   (<u>CID</u>, C_NAME, CREDITS)

The new relational table generated during the N:M conversion—the intersection table—is named ENROLL. The primary key or identifier for the ENROLL table is a concatenated key consisting of CID and SID. Figure 3.5 illustrates how primary key posting works for N:M relationships.

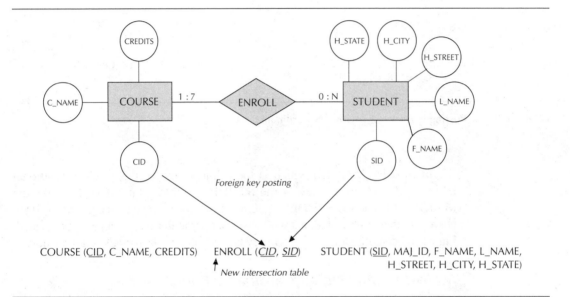

COURSE (<u>CID</u>, C_NAME, CREDITS)   ENROLL (<u>*CID*</u>, <u>*SID*</u>)   STUDENT (<u>SID</u>, MAJ_ID, F_NAME, L_NAME,
                                       ↑ New intersection table   H_STREET, H_CITY, H_STATE)

FIGURE 3.5   Posting Foreign Keys with N:M Cardinality

The relationship between the FACULTY entity and the COURSE entity is also N:M because the relationship from COURSE to FACULTY is *optional* and it has an upper cardinality bound of one (0:1). Recall that *optional* relationships, which have a "one" as the upper cardinality bound, are temporarily labeled as a "many" (N). The business rules for these two entities are:

A faculty member can teach from zero to four courses.

A course can be taught by zero or one faculty members.

Converting the N:M relationship between FACULTY and COURSE results in the following relational tables:

FACULTY   (<u>FID</u>, F_NAME, L_NAME)
TEACH   (<u>*FID*</u>, <u>*CID*</u>)
COURSE   (<u>CID</u>, C_NAME, CREDITS)

The new intersection table created as a result of the N:M cardinality is called TEACH. The primary key or identifier for the TEACH table is a concatenated key consisting of the foreign keys FID and CID. Figure 3.6 illustrates how primary key posting works for the FACULTY and COURSE entities, where optional participation on one side causes the relationship to be treated as an N:M during schema mapping.

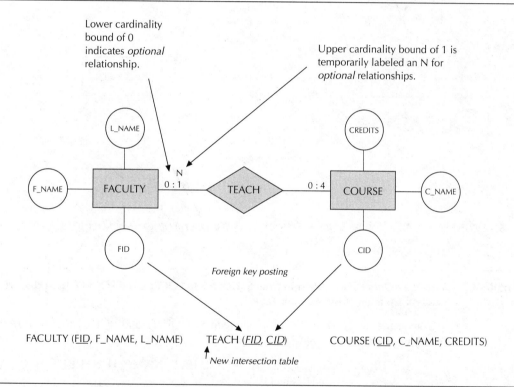

FIGURE 3.6   *Optional* **Relationship from COURSE to FACULTY Results in Creation of Intersection Table**

The relationship between STUDENT and LOCKER is also treated as a many-to-many relationship because of the optional cardinality mapping from STUDENT to LOCKER and from LOCKER to STUDENT. The ER diagram has been temporarily relabeled from a 1 to an N for the upper cardinality bounds. This is necessary in order to convert the ER diagram to the proper relational table configuration. An intersection table called ASSIGN is created to maintain the proper linkage between students and lockers (see Figure 3.7). The business rules for these two entities are:

A student is assigned no locker or one locker.

A locker is assigned to no student or one student.

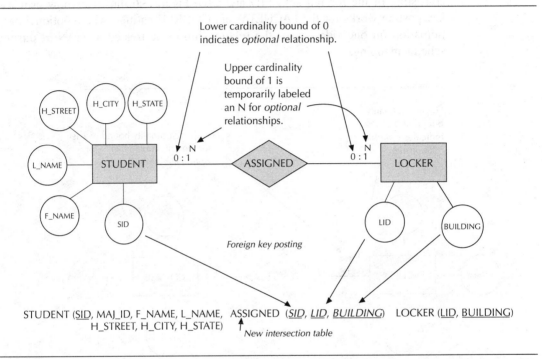

FIGURE 3.7 Two-Way *Optional* Relationship from STUDENT to LOCKER and LOCKER to STUDENT Leads to Creation of Intersection Table

Converting the N:M relationship between STUDENT and LOCKER results in the following relational tables:

STUDENT   (<u>SID</u>, *MAJ_ID*, F_NAME, L_NAME, H_STREET, H_CITY, H_STATE)

ASSIGNED   (<u>SID</u>, *<u>LID</u>*, *<u>BUILDING</u>*)

LOCKER   (<u>LID</u>, <u>BUILDING</u>)

At this point, the conversion from the ER model to relational tables is complete. The labeling of the upper bound as a "many" when an entity is optional is only temporary. In fact, after you use the *optional-max* approach a few times, you will very likely get a feel for how to convert ER diagrams containing optional relationships to relational tables and will no longer have to relabel the diagram.

CONVERTING Isa AND INHERITANCE STRUCTURES TO RELATIONAL TABLES

Figure 3.8 illustrates an *Isa* relationship for students, where graduates and undergraduates inherit attributes of the student entity. The entity supertype or superclass for STUDENT consists of the attributes SID, F_NAME, L_NAME, SEX, and AGE. Entity subtypes for STUDENT include GRADUATE and UNDERGRADUATE. Thus, as we discussed in Chapter 2, GRADUATE *Isa* subclass of STUDENT, and UNDERGRADUATE *Isa* subclass of STUDENT. These subclasses inherit all the attributes for STUDENT, but they also have additional unique attributes. Graduate students, for instance, might have additional attributes indicating whether they passed their qualifying exams or completed their thesis requirement. In contrast, undergraduate students might have additional attributes for the location of their dorm room or their involvement in social fraternities and clubs.

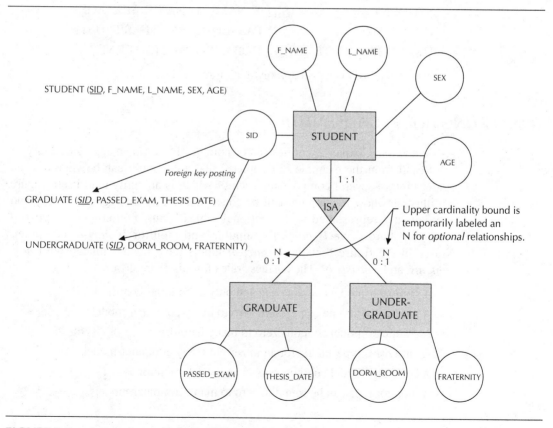

FIGURE 3.8   Converting *Isa* Relationships to Relational Tables

Converting an *Isa* relationship to relational tables is very straightforward when the *optional-max* rules are used. The relationships from STUDENT to GRADUATE and from STUDENT to UNDERGRADUATE have an optional lower bound and a "one" for the upper bound (0:1). In contrast, there is a *mandatory* relationship from GRADUATE to STUDENT and from UNDERGRADUATE to STUDENT, with a lower bound of one and an upper bound of one (1:1). In other words, if an individual is an undergraduate or graduate, then that individual must be a student; however, a student could be either an undergraduate or graduate student. The primary key for STUDENT (SID) is simply posted to the subclasses GRADUATE and UNDERGRADUATE to maintain the proper linkages. Using the *optional-max* approach, the relationships from STUDENT to GRADUATE and from STUDENT to UNDERGRADUATE are both treated as a 1:N upper cardinality bound (see rule 7).

The following tables result from converting the *Isa* relationship in Figure 3.8:

STUDENT   (SID, F_NAME, L_NAME, SEX, AGE)
GRADUATE   (SID, PASSED_EXAM, THESIS_DATE)
UNDERGRADUATE   (SID, DORM_ROOM, FRATERNITY)

Notice that SID is a primary key in all three tables.

CONVERTING AGGREGATE ENTITIES

As we noted in Chapter 2, entities can be combined to form an aggregate entity.

Recall from the example in Chapter 2 that a computer can be viewed as an aggregation of several components, each of which is an entity unto itself. Figure 3.9 illustrates how a computer can be conceptualized as an aggregate entity and subsequently represented with relational tables. Thus motherboard *Is-part-of* computer, hard drive *Is-part-of* computer, and monitor *Is-part-of* computer. Notice in the figure that the *Is-part-of* labels have been replaced with *has*, *contains*, and *consists-of*. The business rules for this example are:

A computer model contains one and only one motherboard.

A motherboard type can exist in zero to many computer models.

A computer model contains zero to many hard drives.

A hard drive type can be found in zero to many computer models.

A computer model contains one and only one monitor.

A monitor type can be found in zero to many computer models.

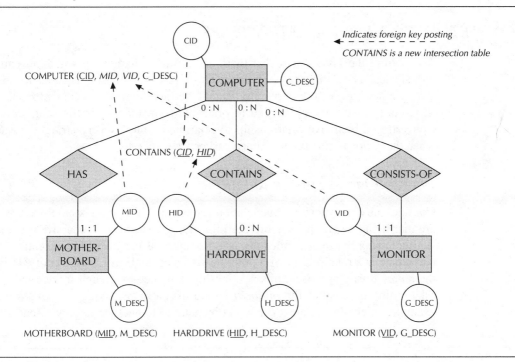

FIGURE 3.9   Converting Entity Aggregations to Relational Tables

For this example, let's imagine that a particular company sells 30 or so models of computers. Each computer must have a motherboard type and a graphics card. The company will equip some computers with only one hard drive, others with many hard drives (file servers), and still others without any hard drive (a diskless workstation).

Once the ER diagram for these relationships is labeled with upper and lower cardinality bounds, the *optional-max* approach can be used to define the relational tables. The primary keys for the MOTHERBOARD and MONITOR are posted to COMPUTER. The primary keys for COMPUTER and HARDDRIVE are posted to a new intersection table called CONTAINS. The following relational tables represent the aggregation of the three *Is-part-of* entities:

COMPUTER   (CID, MID, VID, C_DESC, ...)
MOTHERBOARD   (MID, M_DESC, ...)
CONTAINS   (CID, HID)
HARDDRIVE   (HID, H_DESC, ...)
MONITOR   (VID, G_DESC, ...)

Recall from the last chapter that there are certain situations in which an entity participates in a relationship with itself. This type of relationship is called a recursive relationship, or loop structure. Remember also that in a recursive relationship, entity instances are related to other entity instances for the same entity. Converting a recursive relationship to relational tables is very straightforward when the *optional-max* rules outlined earlier are invoked.

One-to-One Recursive Relationships

Consider the case where an organization wants the ability to track employees who are married to each other. Figure 3.10 illustrates this as a 1:1 recursive relationship involving *optional* entities because instances of the EMPLOYEE entity can participate in a relationship with other instances of the EMPLOYEE entity. Using the *optional-max* approach, this relationship is treated as though it were an N:N relationship because of the *optional* nature of marriage among employees. For example, an employee may or may not be married to another employee, but if an

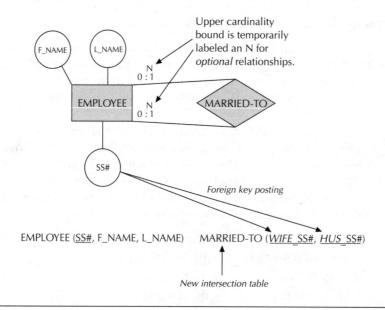

FIGURE 3.10   1:1 Recursive Relationship

employee is married to another employee, that employee can be married to only one other employee (0:1). Converting the N:N recursive relationship using the *optional-max* approach would result in the following relational tables:

EMPLOYEE　　　(SS#, NAME)

MARRIED-TO　　(*WIFE_SS#, HUS_SS#*)

Notice that the primary key (SS#) for the EMPLOYEE entity is in effect posted twice to the new intersection table (MARRIED-TO) to maintain the necessary linkage within the EMPLOYEE table.

Be aware that the 1:1 recursive relationship is not always easy to identify during the ER modeling process. In addition, the procedure for converting recursive relationships into relational tables, particularly *optional* relationships, is not always intuitive on first inspection. The database designer needs to be vigilant of the occurrence of the optional recursive relationships during requirements analysis and use the *optional-max* rules to ensure that the proper relational tables are identified.

One-to-Many Recursive Relationships

The 1:N case for recursive relationships typically occurs when there is a hierarchical one-to-many mapping between entity occurrences for the same entity. The employee and supervisor relationship is a typical example, where an individual supervises many employees, but an employee has only one supervisor. The ER diagram for the 1:N recursive relationship is illustrated in Figure 3.11. Converting the 1:N recursive relationship using the *optional-max* approach would result in the following relational table:

EMPLOYEE　　(SS#, *SUPER_SS#*, F_NAME, L_NAME, ...)

Notice that the primary key (SS#) is posted as a foreign key to the EMPLOYEE table as SUPER_SS#, the same table whence it came. This is the result of using the *optional-max* approach, but it is also necessary in order to maintain the proper database navigation linkages.

Many-to-Many Recursive Relationships

Manufacturing environments often contain N:M recursive relationships among the various parts and subassemblies. This is referred to as the *bill-of-materials relationship*. A bill-of-materials relationship occurs whenever there is a hierarchical structural relationship involving some types of components. In a many-to-many, bill-of-materials situation, a component can have many subcomponents, and a subcomponent can be used in many different components. Figure 3.12 presents the ER diagram for the bill-of-materials relationship.

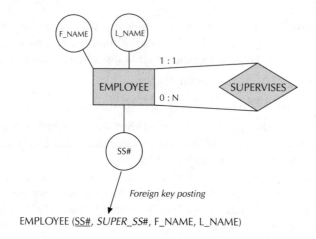

EMPLOYEE (SS#, *SUPER_SS#*, F_NAME, L_NAME)

FIGURE 3.11   1:N Recursive Relationships

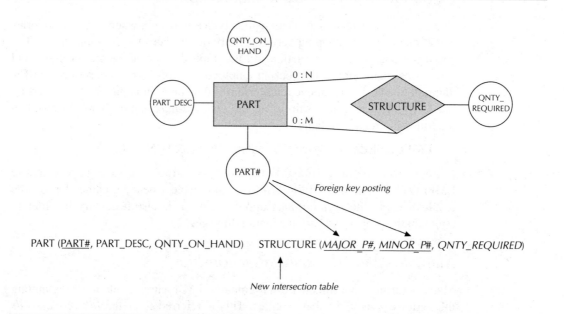

FIGURE 3.12   N:M Recursive Relationships

Using the *optional-max* approach to convert the ER diagram having the N:M recursive relationship results in the following relational tables:

PART   (PART#, PART_DESC)
STRUCTURE   (*MAJOR_P#*, *MINOR_P#*, *QNTY_REQUIRED*)

The new intersection table labeled STRUCTURE is necessary because the cardinality relationship between parts is N:M. The primary key for this table is created by posting the primary key twice from the PARTS entity. Note that the table definition is similar to the definition for the EMPLOYEE MARRIED-TO EMPLOYEE structure.

The following example illustrates the types of records that would populate these relational tables. This particular example relates to an organization that assembles both bicycles and tricycles.

Part Table

Structure Table

PART#	PART_DES	QNTY_ON_HAND	MAJOR_P#	MINOR_P#	QNTY_REQUIRED
A	Bike Frame	100	A	C	1
B	Trike Frame	160	A	G	1
C	Fr. Wheel	90	A	E	1
D	Spokes	2000	B	C	1
E	Chain	88	B	H	1
F	Links	10000	B	E	1
G	Bike Back Wheel	150	C	D	80
H	Trike Back Wheel	125	G	D	80
			H	D	40
			E	F	200

The N:M recursive relationship in this example can also be conceptualized in terms of the *Is-part-of* structure. Thus, SPOKE *Is-part-of* WHEEL and WHEEL *Is-part-of* BIKE FRAME. Or in more general terms, PART *Is-part-of* PART.

TERNARY RELATIONSHIPS

Up to this point, all the ER modeling examples involved relationships in which only two entities were connected to the relationship symbol. When only two entities are connected to a relationship, the relationship is referred to as a **binary**

relationship. When three entities participate in a relationship, it is referred to as a **ternary relationship**; when three or more entities participate in a relationship, it is generically referred to as an **n-ary relationship**. In practice, most ternary relationships and relationships of a higher order can be converted to binary relationships; there are instances, however, when the ternary relationship is the most appropriate way to model a system.

Consider a company (see Figure 3.13) that can supply an inventory item to a customer from one of many warehouses. If it is company policy to link all the customer attributes with item attributes and the warehouse location, the relationship could be modeled as a ternary relationship.

Converting the ER representation to relational tables using the *optional-max* approach results in four tables: the CUSTOMER table, the ITEM table, the WARE-HOUSE table, and the new intersection table ORDERS. This new intersection table

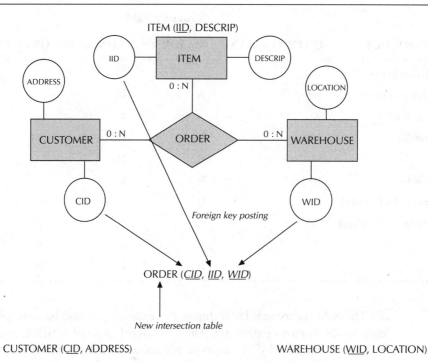

FIGURE 3.13   Ternary Relationship

permits database navigation with the assistance of a concatenated key comprised of the three entity identifiers (CID, IID, and WID). Ternary and higher order relationships are almost always N:N:N, and therefore, the creation of a new intersection table is necessary.

The resulting relational tables for the ternary relationship are:

CUSTOMER   (<u>CID</u>, ADDRESS)
ITEM   (<u>IID</u>, DESCRIP)
WAREHOUSE   (<u>WID</u>, LOCATION)
ORDER   (<u>*CID*</u>, <u>*IID*</u>, <u>*WID*</u>)

PERFORMANCE VERSUS FLEXIBILITY IN DATABASE DESIGN

There are two conflicting objectives in designing relational databases. The first objective is to minimize data anomalies and the presence of null values in relational tables. The use of ER modeling with the accompanying *optional-max* approach will minimize the presence of null values and result in a more stable database. A second objective of database administrators and users—one that is not always articulated—is to minimize the number of relational tables that are created.

When the upper cardinality bounds are, say, 1:2 or 1:3, many database designers simply post the many entity attributes to the one entity. For example, if an employee has three phone numbers (home, office, and cellular), the attributes HOME_PHONE, OFFICE_PHONE, CELLULAR_PHONE are posted to the EMPLOYEE table. In most organizations, there would, however, be null values in the database because some employees would undoubtedly be missing a cellular number. Database design purists would opt for the creation of a relational table to handle the multivalued occurrence of phone numbers.

Similarly, suppose that a student could participate in one, two, or three clubs, and a club could have many students. Rather than create an intersection entity (see Figure 3.14), the attributes CID1, CID2, and CID3 are posted to the STUDENT table. There will, of course, be nulls in the STUDENT table because not all students participate in clubs. It will also be difficult to generate the member list for student clubs using this type of database structure. However, some users and database administrators prefer to organize the information in this way despite such potential problems.

There is often a trade-off between database complexity and flexibility. Creating a new table is correct from a theoretical view—according to the tenets of relational database theory and from a practical standpoint because it is easier to manipulate tables rather than manipulate separate fields. But because there is a downside to creating new tables, some database administrators and users are willing to forgo good design for reasons of performance and simplicity.

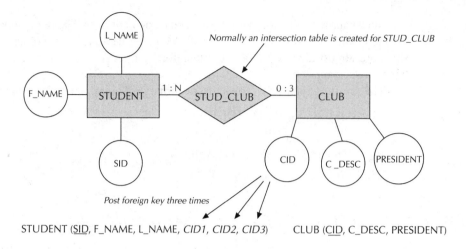

STUDENT (<u>SID</u>, F_NAME, L_NAME, *CID1, CID2, CID3*)   CLUB (<u>CID</u>, C_DESC, PRESIDENT)

FIGURE 3.14   Performance Trade-off

Database administrators argue persuasively that table proliferation affects overall system performance and increases system complexity. Adding tables can degrade the efficiency of data retrieval and manipulation, it can contribute to the amount of time the data administrator spends trying to maintain the database, and it requires more sophisticated end users to access and manipulate the data.

The relationship between STUDENT and LOCKER in Figure 3.15 further illustrates the trade-off between performance and complexity. Because the relationship is *optional* in both directions, that is, from STUDENT to LOCKER and from LOCKER to STUDENT, a new intersection table should be created to match the students to their lockers. The following tables are thus needed to reflect the relationship:

STUDENT   (<u>SID</u>, *MAJ_ID*, F_NAME, L_NAME, H_STREET, H_CITY, H_STATE)

ASSIGNED   (*<u>SID</u>, <u>LID</u>, BUILDING*)

LOCKER   (<u>LID</u>, BUILDING)

The ASSIGNED table can be eliminated by either posting the locker identifier (LID) to STUDENT or posting SID to the LOCKER table. In this case, if we post SID to LOCKER the relational tables would be:

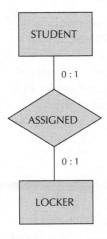

FIGURE 3.15   STUDENT and LOCKER Relationship

STUDENT   (<u>SID</u>, *MAJ_ID*, F_NAME, L_NAME, H_STREET, H_CITY, H_STATE)

LOCKER   (<u>LID</u>, <u>BUILDING</u>, *SID*)

If there are more students than lockers, SID should be posted to LOCKER, and if there are more lockers than students, LID and BUILDING should be posted to STUDENT. This strategy will minimize the number of nulls in the database; however, nulls will be fully minimized *only* when an intersection table is created for the ASSIGNED relationship.

In many instances, organizations are willing to accept a few null values rather than define a new table.

SUMMARY

In the last two chapters, we presented the basic mechanics of ER modeling. This chapter focused on how the ER model can be converted to relational tables. In particular, we illustrated how the *optional-max* approach utilizes the upper and lower cardinality bounds to define the relational tables. We also illustrated how recursive relationships and ternary relationships can be converted to the relational schema. Finally, we discussed the trade-off between minimizing null values and minimizing the proliferation of tables and noted that some database administrators, at the request of users, opt for fewer tables.

The ER modeling approach is very powerful and flexible. This flexibility, however, needs to be complemented with data modeling experience. Instead of experience, there are ways to understand the power behind this tool by examining ER models. The appendix following this chapter is devoted to examples of ER applications. In addition, examples in various database books and trade publications can be used to facilitate the data modeling process.

Review Questions

1. Explain the *optional-max* process for converting an ER diagram to relational tables. What is the benefit of using this conversion process?

2. Discuss the advantages and disadvantages of minimizing null values versus creating new tables in database design.

Example 1: Valery's Gallery Order Processing System

Valery's Gallery of Gourmet Gifts is a catalog mail-order company specializing in up-scale kitchen tools and utensils. Fast order processing is essential for mail-order firms to compete effectively, and Valery's Gallery is no exception. The following description details Valery's current manual order processing system

Val currently employs two people to handle all the phone and mail orders. A sample order form from one of Valery's current catalogs is illustrated in Figure 3.16. When an order is received in the mail, it is examined by one of the two order processing personnel to determine if the credit card information is valid and if the catalog item is available. Product availability is determined by inspecting the Master CATALOG (see Figure 3.17). The available quantity is updated by hand on the catalog by crossing out the old quantity and replacing it with the updated quantity. Phone orders are handwritten by the sales personnel right on an order form, then validated during slack periods. All invalid orders, whether they are written or phoned in, are returned to the customer via next-day mail. The valid orders are then placed in a box labeled ORDERS and processed at night by the shipping department.

There are five individuals in the shipping department who fill orders on a first-come, first-served basis. To fill the order, one of the shipping department employees takes an order out of the ORDERS box, then walks around the warehouse and retrieves each item that is on the order form. A handwritten packing slip is created as the items are retrieved from inventory. The ordered items and packing slip are then packed in the appropriate size shipping containers and sent to the customer. The data flow diagram (DFD) for Valery's current order processing system is illustrated in Figure 3.18.[1]

---

[1] There are, of course, additional detailed operational activities that take place at Valery's, such as updating the master inventory catalog for the number of units to deduct from the quantity on hand, but the details of these processes have been excluded from the discussion in order to simplify the example.

Order Form

Order Toll Free 1-800-323-4242
Credit card holders may order 24 hours a day, 7 days a week.
By Fax: call 1-708-480-8929

SHIP TO:
If the address is a P.O. Box, please fill in a local street address in the
section below so that we may deliver via UPS.

Name ___Deborah Smith_____

Address ___100 Main Street_____

City __Boston_____ State __MA_____ Zip _55555_

(617) 555-1111

Daytime Phone (Required to process order)

Catalog #	How Many	Catalog Description	Price	Total Price Dollars	Cents
1956	1	Open Up Jar Opener	29.99	29	99
6871	2	Henckels 2-1/4" Peeling Knife	19.99	39	98
2987	1	Scoop Colander	19.95	19	95

Method of Payment:

☑ Check/Money Order   ☐ Visa
☐ MasterCard   ☐ Discover

Card Number #

_____

Note: Your credit card is charged after
your merchandise is shipped

Authorized Signature (Sign below)

	Dollars	Cents
Merchandise Total	89	92
Sales Tax All Shipments to IL. add 7% tax	4	49
Shipping & Insurance (Use chart below)	6	95
UPS 2nd Day Air $5.95 more!		
Total in U.S. Funds (no stamps or cash)	101	36

Guaranteed Safe Delivery

Total Order:	ADD:
Up to $10	3.95
10.01 to 30	5.95
30.01 to 50	6.95
50.01 to 80	9.95
80.01 to 110	11.95
110.01 to 160	13.95
Over 160	16.95

FIGURE 3.16   Sample Order Form

Master Catalog
Valery's Gallery of Gourmet Gifts

Catalog #	Catalog Description	Price	Quantity on Hand
1718	Calphalon 14" Pizza Pan	$29.99	23
2869	Sabatier Grand Chef Block Set	$279.00	9
2053	Fefal Cool Wall Super Deep Fryer	$109.99	8
3141	1/2 Gallon Professional Bar Mixer	$195.00	13
1956	Open Up Jar Opener	$29.99	22
2678	Deluxe Can Opener	$34.95	27
1490	Chopping Bowl Set	$11.99	30
2313	Vertical Steamer	$19.99	28
5716	Bosch Coffee Grinder	$69.99	25
2269	The Swinger	$49.99	30
4964	In-Drawer Knife Tray	$29.99	32
6871	Henckels 2-1/4" Peeling Knife	$19.99	44
1303	Ravioli Maker	$13.95	29
2987	Scoop Colander	$19.95	16
2171	Deep Dish Pizza Set	$19.99	29
1879	Krups Toastronic Signal Toaster	$69.99	4
2616	Good Grips Swivel Peeler	$9.95	41
0402	Bar-B-Chek	$19.95	24
0762	Farberware Convection/Broil Oven	$265.00	20
1483	Gingerbread House Mold	$19.95	27
5087	Wok Topper	$14.99	14
3173	Non-stick Oven Pancake Pan	$17.99	13
2657	DietMate Computer	$295.00	10
2991	Mini Angel Food Rack	$21.95	15
1781	Organizer Cart	$139.95	23
4211	Krispy Kan	$12.99	29

FIGURE 3.17   **Master Catalog**

Tremendous market demand for products, coupled with delays in filling orders, has prompted Valery's chief executive officer to consider installing a local area network along with a relational database management system.

The ER diagram for the automated order processing system is depicted in Figure 3.19. The relational table definitions that follow were derived using the *optional-max* approach. Composite attributes have been converted to simple attributes (for example, customer name), primary keys are underlined, and foreign keys are in

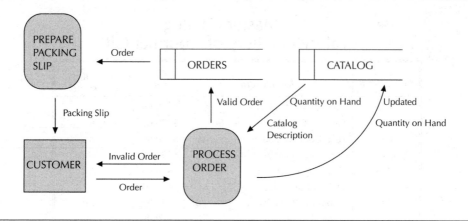

FIGURE 3.18   A Data Flow Diagram for Valery's Gallery

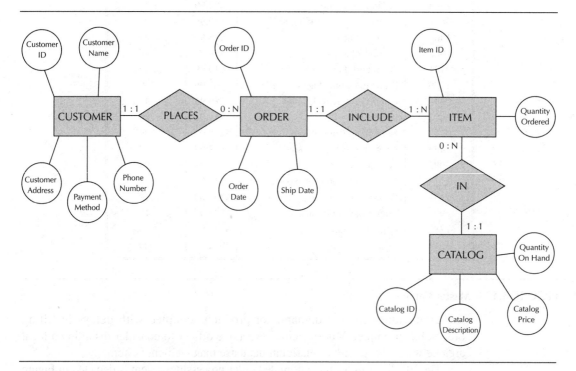

FIGURE 3.19   An ER Diagram for Valery's Gallery

italics. The relational tables for Valery's Gallery order processing systems are as follows:

CUSTOMER	(<u>CID</u>, F_NAME, L_NAME, ST_ADDRESS, CITY, STATE, ZIP, PHONE, CREDIT_CARD_TYPE, CARD_NUMBER)
ORDER	(<u>OID</u>, *CID* ORDER_DATE, SHIP_DATE)
ITEM	(<u>IID</u>, *OID, CAT_ID*, QUANTITY_ORDERED)
CATALOG	(<u>CAT_ID</u>, DESCRIPTION, PRICE, QTY_ON_HAND)

When constructing an ER diagram, the systems analyst can interview users and utilize various user documents and systems documentation to identify the entities. In general, the order form for Valery's Gallery and the master catalog listing were used. In this example, any input or output of the current system can be used to identify entities. For example, the name, address, phone, and credit card information from the order form in Figure 3.16 could be used as the initial attributes for the CUSTOMER entity. You can actually just take a document and indicate with a pen which attributes should be attached to a particular entity.

Of particular interest is how the data store in the data flow diagram corresponds to the entities on the ER diagram. The order, which comes from the customer in the manual paper-based system and ends up in the ORDERS data store, is actually a complex data object containing attributes that are found in several entities.

Figure 3.20 illustrates that attributes from the order document correspond to

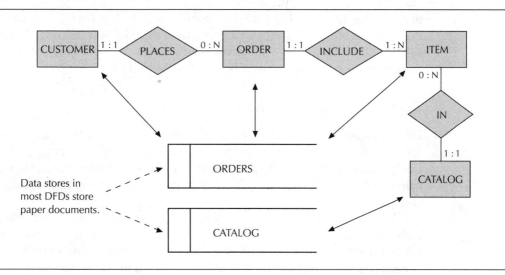

FIGURE 3.20 **A Correspondence Between ORDERS on DFD and the ER Diagram**

the attributes in the CUSTOMER, ORDER, ITEM, and CATALOG entities and that the attributes in the CATALOG data store correspond to the attributes in the CATALOG entity. The CATALOG in the original ER diagram was an actual paper catalog containing inventory information. The catalog in the new system is electronic and is still called a CATALOG, but the information is contained in a relational table.

The order from the customer, whether it is phoned in or called in, is used to add records to the CUSTOMER, ORDER, and ITEM tables. The CATALOG is used to verify item availability and validity and to track the amount of product in inventory (the quantity-on-hand attribute). If a customer has done business with the company before, a new customer record will not be added. The existing customer record in that case will just be updated with any new information.

There is a noticeable degree of similarity between the ER diagram and the DFD diagram. First of all, the data flowing from external entities to processes in a DFD will eventually become entity attributes. In many instances, the data flowing from an external DFD entity is in the form of a paper document, and these paper documents contain attributes that will eventually reside in many different files. You can think of a paper document as a complex aggregate entity that has many parts associated with it.

The confusion between the data store in the data flow diagram and the relational table, as represented in an ER diagram, can be alleviated by drawing DFDs that in some way distinguish data in relational tables from paper data flows. Figure 3.21 shows an example of a modified DFD that incorporates a relational table symbol (the rectangle) and the hard copy representation of the original order that will end up in the ORDERS data store. Notice that the CATALOG data store that was part of the old system is missing from the data flow diagram. The paper catalog can of course be readily produced through a simple query of the electronic catalog, which is now the CATALOG relational table.

Example 2: Duffers Paradise

Duffers Paradise is an 18-hole golf course located in Phoenix, Arizona. The owners of Duffers have decided to computerize certain parts of their operation. In particular, they are interested in automating the course reservation system, the calculation of golfers' handicaps, membership record keeping, and course usage statistics.

To play golf at the course, you must be a member of the Duffers Paradise club. Membership in the club costs $100 per year. When this fee is paid, a membership card is filled out with the appropriate information (Figure 3.22). Nonmembers may play only if they are accompanied by a member.

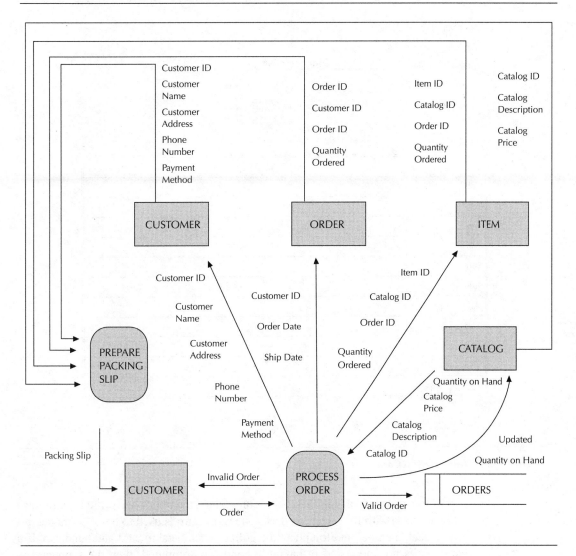

FIGURE 3.21   **A Modified Data Flow Diagram for Valery's Gallery**

To reserve a tee time (a time to play golf), a member calls the club house at the golf course and arranges an available time slot with the reception desk. The reception desk reserves the tee time by writing the member's name and the number of players in the party on the course schedule (see Figure 3.23).

When a member arrives at the course, he or she checks in at the reception desk and pays the greens fee. Nonmembers who are escorted by a member must also check in and pay a greens fee.

Member Identification _3056_

Member Name _____Mark Denton_____

Member Address _____18 Scoutfire Way_____

Month	Golfing Activity
Jan	ⴸⴸ ‖
Feb	‖‖
Mar	ⴸⴸ ‖‖‖
Apr	‖
May	ⴸⴸ ⴸⴸ ⴸⴸ
Jun	‖‖‖
Jul	ⴸⴸ
Aug	‖
Sep	ⴸⴸ ⴸⴸ
Oct	‖
Nov	‖‖‖
Dec	‖‖

Date Paid _____1/15/95_____

FIGURE 3.22   Membership Card

After a round of golf has been completed, members leave their score card (Figure 3.24) with the reception desk. The score card is used to track golfing activity of each member and to update the golfer's membership card and handicap. If a member is not interested in having a handicap computed, then the scorecard is turned in with only the member's name and no score. Members receive an updated copy of their new handicap (Figure 3.25) on a monthly basis. The owners of Duffers receive daily, weekly, and monthly reports indicating golf course utilization statistics such as how many members play each day, week, and month and who plays the most golf each month.

The data flow diagrams for Duffers' system is illustrated in Figure 3.26. This is a simplified view of a golf course business, but it reflects Duffers' business rules

Date **2/1/95**

Time	Party Name
6:00 AM	Hill (3)
6:15 AM	Johnson (4)
6:30 AM	Denton (3)
6:45 AM	Miller (1)
7:00 AM	~~Parton~~ (2) canceled
7:15 AM	Sing (3)
7:30 AM	Newman (3)
7:45 AM	Orrange (2)
8:00 AM	Vian (1)
8:15 AM	Temple (3)
8:30 AM	Harvey (4)
...	

FIGURE 3.23 **Duffers' Course Registration Sheet**

and the way the owners want to run their golf course. The resulting database necessary to run the business as described is very simple, as illustrated in Figure 3.27. Only two relational tables are needed to capture data on the MEMBER entity and GOLF entity. The member identifier would be posted to each instance of GOLF to maintain the 1:N PLAY relationship. Composite attributes have been converted to simple attributes (for example, customer name), primary keys are underlined, and foreign keys are in italics. The relational tables for Duffers follow:

MEMBER (MID, F_NAME, L_NAME, ST_ADDRESS, CITY, STATE, ZIP, DATE_PAID)

GOLF (DATE, TIME, MID, SCORE)

The membership card, the handicap, and various course utilization reports for management could be readily generated with these two files.

Date _____

Name	1	2	3	4	5	6	7	8	9	FRONT 9 TOTAL
Denton	3	4	5	5	3	4	3	4	5	38
Joyce	4	4	4	5	4	4	4	4	3	36
Peterson	4	4	4	5	3	4	5	4	3	37

Name	1	2	3	4	5	6	7	8	9	BACK 9 TOTAL	TOTAL FOR 18
Denton	4	4	4	4	3	4	3	4	4	34	72
Joyce	5	5	6	5	5	6	4	4	4	44	80
Peterson	5	7	5	4	5	5	6	5	4	46	83

FIGURE 3.24   Duffers' Scorecard

Member Name _____Mark Denton_____

Member Identification Number ____3056____

Handicap _____2_____   Date Calculated ____2/1/95____

FIGURE 3.25   Duffers' Handicap

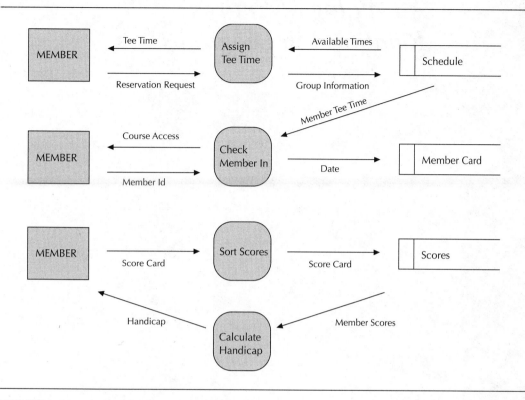

FIGURE 3.26   Duffers' Data Flow Diagram

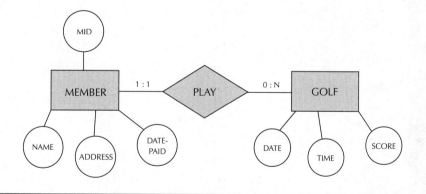

FIGURE 3.27   Duffers' ER Diagram

4

A Catalog of Entity Relationship Diagrams

In this chapter, we present several examples of entity relationship diagrams. The examples in this chapter were adapted from a variety of sources, including consulting projects, textbooks from the various functional areas (accounting, marketing, production, human resources, and so forth), articles in professional publications, and MBA student projects.

The ER diagrams in this chapter can be used to gain further insight into ER modeling concepts, but they can also be a starting point and reference for database design in a particular application area. The ER diagrams are accompanied by relational table definitions that contain examples of primary keys and their related attributes. Primary keys or identifiers for the relational tables are underlined, and foreign keys are italicized. The suffix, ID, along with some combination of letters from the entity name is used to construct the name for the primary key or identifier (for example, CUST_ID or CID). The attributes in the relational tables are a combination of atomic attributes (for example, FIRST_NAME and LAST_NAME) and composite attributes (for example, CUSTOMER_ NAME).

You are encouraged to examine the upper and lower cardinality bounds for each application in order to determine the business rules that are in effect for the particular organization. The *optional-max* approach, discussed in Chapter 3, was used to convert the ER diagrams to relational tables.

HUMAN RESOURCES

Human Resources (HR) deals with issues such as staffing, compensation, employee evaluation, employee training, and career development. In the past, the HR function has been slower to computerize than other functional areas because the financial accounting, operations, and marketing functions have been given greater priority in the assignment of computing resources. This is now changing because employees are being viewed as a strategic resource who represent a vast pool of skills and knowledge distributed throughout the organization. Organizations can draw on this pool of expertise to match skills to organizational tasks, to locate individuals with unique and specialized skills, and to cultivate the employee resource pool by providing education and training programs. Matching skills to projects and providing the ability to search for expertise looms as a very critical, strategic HR application in the next decade, and it will require some type of centralized integrated database.

One area in which there is a significant amount of pressure for applications development is in the benefits management area. In a so-called cafeteria benefit plan, employees are given a fixed dollar amount that they can use to select from a variety of benefits options. In this way, employees can select the level of benefits, such as hospital coverage, dental coverage, death benefits, and disability insurance, that best fits their needs. These systems require more processing power and additional reporting mechanisms than traditional benefits systems.

A generic ER diagram that could be readily adapted to address several needs of the human resource function is illustrated in Figure 4.1. Several interesting aspects of the ER diagram will be pointed out. First of all, there is a recursive relationship labeled SUPERVISES, where the business rule states that supervisors must supervise at least one employee and that employees must have a supervisor. Using the *optional-max* approach for conversion dictates that the primary key for the supervisor should be posted to the employee table. Additional discussion of recursive relationships can be found in Chapter 2.

Note that the intersection table PARENT-OF is necessary for linking the EMPLOYEE and DEPENDENT tables because employees can be married to one another, and therefore, a dependent can have two parents working in the same organization. Additional insight into the business rules used to construct this diagram can be determined by examining the cardinality relationship among the entities. The relational tables for the ER diagram in Figure 4.1 are as follows:

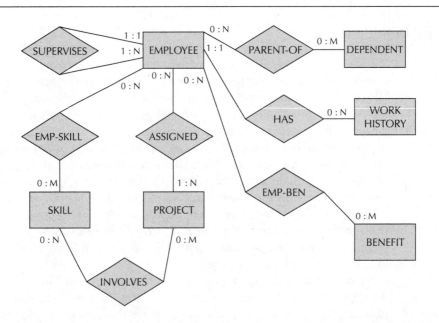

FIGURE 4.1   ER Diagram for Human Resources

EMPLOYEE	(EID, *SUPERVISOR_EID*, NAME, ADDRESS)
EMP-SKILL	(*EID*, *SKILL_ID*)
SKILL	(SKILL_ID, SKILL_DESCRIPTION)
PARENT-OF	(*EID*, *DEPENDENT_ID*)
DEPENDENT	(DEPENDENT_ID, DEPENDENT_NAME)
WORK-HISTORY	(DATE_OF_WORK, *EID*, WORK_DESCRIPTION)
EMP-BEN	(*EID*, *BID*)
BENEFIT	(BID, BENEFIT_DESCRIPTION)
ASSIGNED	(*EID*, *PID*)
PROJECT	(PID, PROJECT_DESCRIPTION)
INVOLVES	(*SKILL_ID*, *PID*)

TECHNICAL SUPPORT AND MAINTENANCE SUPPORT

Technical support and maintenance support are becoming an increasingly important part of customer service. There are two primary activities in technical and maintenance support. The first activity is problem classification and tracking, which involves entering the problem specifics and symptoms into a problem tracking database, classifying the problem, and initiating the process of solving the problem. The second activity in technical and maintenance support is problem resolution, which involves many activities, including directing the customer to the proper technical support personnel, replacing a damaged or inadequate service with a new product or service, sending a technician to the customer site to repair a product or to repeat a service, and scheduling periodic preventive maintenance visits. Some examples of technical and maintenance support follow.

Taxpayer Assistance

When taxpayers have problems filling out their income tax return, they can call the Taxpayer Services Division of the Internal Revenue Service, where their problems are assigned to a tax specialist. The number of phone calls from taxpayers has increased dramatically in recent years, and the IRS is working to maintain high response levels on phone calls that require additional research. The current system is a manual, paper-based system. The accompanying ER diagram in Figure 4.2, which was designed as part of a student project and has not been implemented as of this writing, would be implemented with terminals or PCs connected to a centralized database. Relational tables and attributes that reflect the system essentials for the ER diagram in Figure 4.2 follow:

TAXPAYER	(<u>TAXPAYER_NAME</u>, PHONE, ADDRESS)
INQUIRY	(<u>INQUIRY_ID</u>, *TAXPAYER_NAME,* *SPECIALISTS_NAME,* INQUIRY_DATE, QUESTION {*inquiry*}, INQUIRY_CATEGORY, ANSWER {*how resolved*}, RESOLUTION_DATE, TAX_LAW_REFERENCE)
SPECIALIST	(<u>SPECIALISTS_NAME</u>)

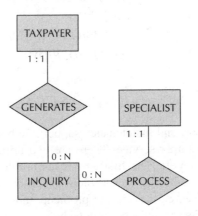

FIGURE 4.2   **Taxpayer Assistance**

Information Systems Technical Support

This example involves a large hospital with a mainframe and minicomputer connected to over 500 terminals and over 200 printers. When users at the hospital encounter problems with hardware or software applications, they call the hospital's technical support staff for assistance. The current system is manual and paper driven and revolves around what is referred to as a "problem log." Each problem in the problem log is assigned to an individual (RESOLVER) who has the responsibility of resolving the problem. The development of a "Help Desk" function, along with a central database, was proposed as a way to reduce response time, reduce paperwork, centralize problem resolution, and ensure followup.

In this example, shown in Figure 4.3, there are three problem subclasses: on-line, batch, and hardware. These are each linked to the PROBLEM entity by an *Isa* structure. According to the *optional-max* approach, the identifier for the PROBLEM table should be posted to the three specialization tables—ONLINE,

BATCH, and HARDWARE—to implement the *Isa* relationship. Relational tables and attributes that reflect system essentials for the ER diagram in Figure 4.3 follow:

USER	(<u>USER_NAME</u>, USER_DEPARTMENT)
PROBLEM	(<u>PROBLEM_NUMBER</u>, *USER_NAME*, *RESOLVER_NAME,* DATE, TIME, PROBLEM_TYPE, APPLICATION_NAME, PROBLEM_SEVERITY, TIME_OF_FAILURE, HOURS_TO_FIX, DATE_FIXED)
RESOLVER	(<u>RESOLVER_NAME</u>, RESOLVER_OFFICE, PHONE)
ONLINE	(*<u>PROBLEM_NUMBER</u>*, DESCRIPTION)
BATCH	(*<u>PROBLEM-NUMBER</u>*, DESCRIPTION, JOB_NAME, JOB_NUMBER, ERROR-TYPE)
HARDWARE	(*<u>PROBLEM-NUMBER</u>*, DESCRIPTION, EQUIPMENT_ID, EQUIPMENT_TYPE, TELEPHONE_AT_LOCATION)

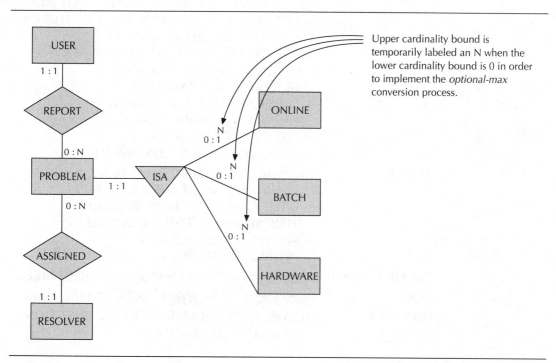

FIGURE 4.3   **Technical Support for Systems**

Machine Maintenance

Supporting customer maintenance needs is an important part of providing customer service. In this example, a large soft drink bottling company wants to provide better maintenance support to its customers who lease over 13,000 soft drink dispensers. In particular, the organization wants to improve machine maintenance, parts inventory management, and management reports. When a customer calls in a problem with a soft drink dispenser (EQUIPMENT), this initiates a repair order (REPAIR). The repair order for the machine is in turn assigned to an individual for repair (REPAIR-PERSON).

The ER diagram for this application is presented in Figure 4.4. Notice how parts that are assigned to a particular repair are also related to items that are in inventory by posting the identifier for the inventory to the part entity. The essential relational tables and attributes for this application are as follows:

CUSTOMER	(<u>CUSTOMER_ACCOUNT_NUMBER</u>, NAME, ADDRESS, PHONE)
EQUIPMENT	(<u>EQUIPMENT_ID</u>, *CUSTOMER_ACCOUNT_NUMBER,* UNIT_SIZE, KEY_NUMBER_TO_OPEN, MANUFACTURER, PURCHASED_FROM, INVOICE#, PURCHASE_DATE, DATE_PUT_IN_SERVICE, CURRENT_METER_READING, CURRENT_READING_DATE, PREVIOUS_METER-READING, PREVIOUS_READING_DATE, DATE_LAST_SERVICED, TYPE_OF_SERVICE_CONTRACT)
REPAIR	(<u>REPAIR_ID</u>, *CUSTOMER_ACCOUNT_NUMBER, EQUIPMENT_ID, REPAIR_PERSON_ID,* DATE_CALLED_IN, DATE_REPAIRED, TIME_ARRIVED, TIME_DEPARTED, PROBLEM_ DESCRIPTION, PROBLEM_CATEGORY)
REPAIR-PERSON	(<u>REPAIR_PERSON_ID</u>, NAME, BEEPER_NUMBER)
PART	(<u>*REPAIR_ID*</u>, <u>*INVENTORY_ID*</u>, QUANTITY_USED)
INVENTORY	(<u>INVENTORY_ID</u>, INVENTORY_DESCRIPTION, QUANTITY_ON-HAND)

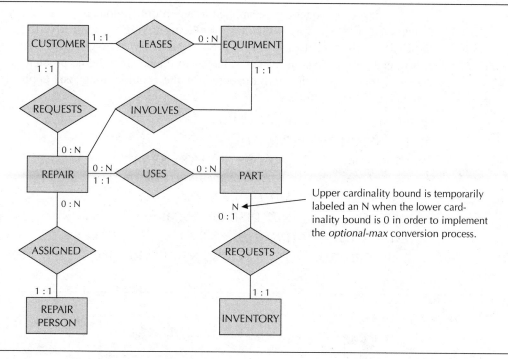

Upper cardinality bound is temporarily labeled an N when the lower cardinality bound is 0 in order to implement the *optional-max* conversion process.

FIGURE 4.4   **Vending Machine Maintenance**

Problem Diagnosis

Up to this point, the discussion has focused primarily on the administrative aspects of technical and maintenance support, such as problem classification, tracking, and followup. Computer-based support for problem diagnosis, however, is where customer support is taken to the next level. An expert system shell with an inference engine is the tool of choice for complex diagnosis applications; however, relational databases can be used as the repository for expertise and provide problem diagnosis support.

Figure 4.5 illustrates a generic ER diagram for diagnosing diseases. Notice that the cardinality bounds provide insight into this particular view of the knowledge domain by indicating that diseases can have zero to many treatments and that a treatment is assigned to at least one disease. In other words, the model suggests that treatments cannot go looking for a disease.

The diagnosis model can be applied to any problem domain where diagnosis is involved. For example, by simply replacing PATIENT with ENGINE, and DISEASE with PROBLEM, and PAT_SYMPTOM with ENG_SYMPTOM, the entity relationship diagram can be adapted to diagnosing engine problems. The essential relational tables and attributes for the problem diagnosis application detailed in Figure 4.5 follow:

PATIENT	(<u>PID</u>, NAME)
PAT-SYMPTOM	(<u>*PID*</u>, <u>*SID*</u>)
SYMPTOM	(<u>SID</u>, DESCRIPTION, SYMPTOM_CATEGORY {*cough, temperature, itch, etc.*})
ASSOCIATE	(<u>*SID*</u>, <u>*DID*</u>)
DISEASE	(<u>DID</u>, DISEASE_NAME)
INDICATES	(<u>*DID*</u>, <u>*TID*</u>)
TREATMENT	(<u>TID</u>, TREATMENT-DESCRIPTION)

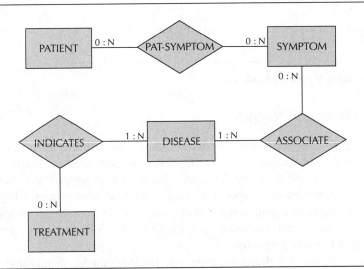

FIGURE 4.5   **Disease Diagnosis**

RESERVATION SYSTEMS

Reservation systems are used to allocate nearly anything you can imagine: tractors, cars, videos, books, rooms, seats at a concert or sporting event, seats on a train, boat, or plane, and campsites, to name a few examples. The notion of time is an important concept in reservation systems because goods and services are leased or rented for a specific period, and time determines when the inventory is consumed.

To illustrate this concept, suppose a plane has 300 seats and the plane is scheduled to fly from New York to Los Angeles one day, and then return to New York the next day. Each flight scheduled generates 300 unique units of seat inventory. In one year, given the foregoing schedule, the plane generates 109,500 (365 days times 300 seats) seat inventory units in a year. As soon as the plane departs from the gate, the 300 inventory units for that flight are immediately consumed, whether or not the seat is occupied by a passenger.

Time can be used to amplify the number of seat units available. For example, the plane can be scheduled to return to New York the same day. This would generate an additional 109,500 units of seat inventory.

The success of American Airlines' Sabre and United Airlines' Apollo reservation systems in providing these companies with a competitive advantage is well known. The complexity and scope of these two systems have preempted market entry, but these databases have also permitted United and American to offer new services. The airline reservation databases provide the central core on which a variety of other services were offered.

At this time, reservation systems for many companies are not just a way to gain a competitive edge. They are also a necessary part of competing in markets where leasing and renting goods or services is the primary business activity. Companies that do not develop their own in-house systems must enter into out-sourcing contracts with companies that specialize in providing reservation services.

Special Events Ticketing

Figure 4.6 illustrates a generic ER diagram for reserving a seat at a sporting event, concert, or play in a multi-use auditorium. Each performance is assigned a unique venue identifier. For example, if *Phantom of the Opera* is scheduled for 30 performances, 30 unique venue identifiers would be assigned to it, one for each performance. Although the performance description and the date and time of the performance could be used as the primary key, many ticket agencies use some sort of unique performance identifier (for example, PID) to delineate the numerous events they handle. Each seat would be uniquely identified by the performance identifier and section, row, and seat number. Therefore, for a performance held in an auditorium containing 1,000 seats, a total of 30,000 units of seat inventory would be generated (30 times 1,000). The relational tables for the ER diagram follow:

CUSTOMER	(CID, ADDRESS, PHONE, PAYMENT_METHOD)
RESERVES	(CID, SECTION, ROW, SEAT, PID)
SEAT-INVENTORY	(SECTION, ROW, SEAT, PID, RESERVATION_STATUS)
PERFORMANCE	(PID, DATE, TIME, DESCRIPTION)

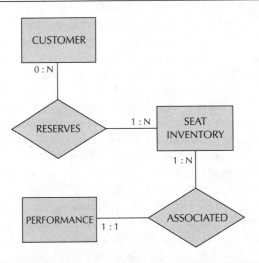

FIGURE 4.6 **Reservation System for Theater, Sporting Event, or Concert**

Hotel and Motel Reservation Systems

Figure 4.7 illustrates a generic ER diagram for a hotel database. In many hotels, a reservation can be made up to a year in advance. Occupancy percentages are computed by counting the number of rooms customers have reserved for a particular date (a simple SQL query). This information is contained in the RESERVES table. Room assignments can be made either the day before or the day of customer arrival. Room assignments are typically controlled by the reservation system with input from management.

The database for the hotel and motel reservation system is very similar to the performance or venue database described earlier. Note that room inventory (ROOM-DAYS) is actually a function of the number of unique rooms and the number of days in a year. Thus a hotel with 100 rooms would have an inventory of 36,500 unique room-days (100 rooms times 365 days). The relational tables for the ER diagram follow:

CUSTOMER	(CID, ADDRESS, PHONE, DATE_OF_ARRIVAL, DATE_OF_DEPARTURE, PAYMENT_METHOD)
RESERVES	(CID, DAY_RESERVED, RID)
ROOM-DAYS	(DAY_RESERVED, RID, RESERVATION_STATUS)
ROOM	(RID, FLOOR, ROOM_NUMBER)

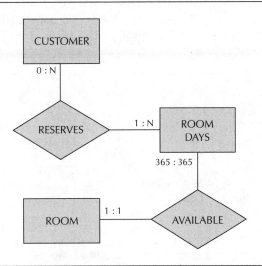

FIGURE 4.7   **Hotel or Motel Reservation**

Airline Reservation Systems

The next example of a reservation system is a flight reservation database. Figure 4.8 illustrates a simple generic flight reservation database. The flight number attribute and the date of the flight are used to construct an identifier for each row in the FLIGHT table. Seats can be thought of as inventory, where each seat is uniquely identified by the row number, the seat number, the flight number, and the flight date. As seats are assigned, seat inventory is in effect reduced. As we noted earlier, all seat inventory is actually consumed when the flight leaves the gate, whether or not there is a revenue-generating passenger occupying the seat.

Utilization statistics can be readily computed for each flight by examining the RESERVES and FLIGHT tables, along with information on aircraft capacities contained in the AIRCRAFT table. The database for the flight reservation system is very similar to the hotel and performance databases. The relational tables for the ER diagram follow:

CUSTOMER	(<u>CID</u>, ADDRESS, PHONE, PAYMENT_METHOD)
RESERVES	(<u>*CID*</u>, <u>*ROW*</u>, <u>*SEAT*</u>, <u>*FLIGHT_NUMBER*</u>, <u>*DATE*</u>)
SEAT-INVENTORY	(<u>ROW</u>, <u>SEAT</u>, <u>*FLIGHT_NUMBER*</u>, <u>*DATE*</u>, RESERVATION_STATUS)
FLIGHT	(<u>FLIGHT_NUMBER</u>, <u>DATE</u>, *TYPE_OF_AIRCRAFT*, ORIGINATION_CITY, DESTINATION_CITY, FLIGHT_DISTANCE, DEPARTURE_TIME, ARRIVAL_TIME)
AIRCRAFT	(<u>TYPE_OF_AIRCRAFT</u>, PASSENGER_CAPACITY)

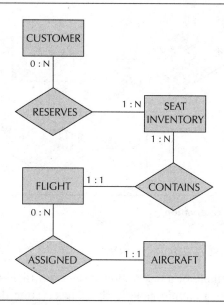

FIGURE 4.8   **Flight Reservation Database**

CHARITIES

Charitable organizations can reap many benefits from a properly designed database. Computer-based systems can assist in tracking and targeting contributors and potential contributors. They can also provide services to donors, such as year-end contribution summaries, to assist them in filing their tax returns. Although there are software packages for maintaining mailing lists and contribution summaries, in some situations there are specialized requirements that require custom development. As is true for many of the applications discussed in this chapter, there are situations where custom database design is the best approach for satisfying organizational information requirements.

A typical ER diagram for a charity is outlined in Figure 4.9. Note the four *Isa* specializations of gifts: stock, property, art, and cash. One of the more interesting aspects of this particular example is that a particular gift could have many instances of property, art, stock, and cash. For example, the gift could include property at several locations. The relational tables for the ER diagram follow:

PATRON	(<u>PID</u>, NAME, ADDRESS, PHONE, CATEGORY, TYPE {*business or private donor*})
DONATES	(<u>*PID*</u>, <u>*GID*</u>)
GIFT	(<u>GID</u>, DATE_GIFT_GIVEN)
STOCK	(<u>STOCK_ID</u>, *GID*, STOCK_NAME, NUMBER_OF_SHARES, CURRENT_PRICE_PER_SHARE)
PROPERTY	(<u>PROP_ID</u>, *GID*, PROP_ADDRESS, CURRENT_PROP_VALUE)
ART	(<u>AID</u>, *GID*, DESCRIPTION, ARTIST, CURRENT_ART_VALUE)
CASH	(<u>CASH_ID</u>, *GID*, AMOUNT)

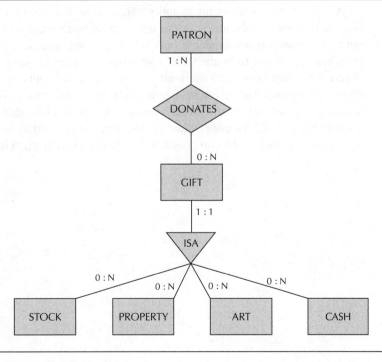

FIGURE 4.9   Charity Database

Fund raising organizations usually attempt to segment patrons by assigning them to categories. The CATEGORY attribute in the PATRON table captures this type of information. For example, a contributor might be classified according to the types of charitable events he or she is interested in. Using these classifications, a patron who likes to participate in athletic activities such as walk-a-thons or bike-a-thons would have the code ATH entered for CATEGORY. On the other hand, an individual who is interested in charitable events centered on cultural activities would have the code ART entered for the CATEGORY attribute. Another entity that might be added to this database would be POTENTIAL-PATRONS. Converting potential patrons to active patronage is an important growth strategy for charities.

PRODUCTION OPERATIONS MANAGEMENT SYSTEMS

Production systems have undergone a dramatic change toward simplicity with the emergence of just-in-time (JIT) inventory and production concepts. Based in large part on customer demand, there is now market pressure to reduce the time it takes to design, produce, and deliver products. Customer demand in a JIT environment can be viewed as pulling or drawing products from companies.

Complex economic order quantity calculations for determining optimal lot sizes have been supplanted with the notion of zero inventory—having the right number of components available only when they are needed. Lot sizes in a JIT plant are not related to mathematical formulas but, instead, are a function of the different Kanban boxes that are used for holding components. In a flexible, synchronized manufacturing environment, the customer-driven master production schedule dictates where and when a component should be delivered. It is the responsibility of the supplier, whether that supplier is internal or external to the organization, to deliver the component to the proper location when it is needed.

Highlight 4.1 *SkyRock ATB*

SkyRock ATB

SkyRock[1] ATB manufactures three different models of all-terrain bicycles. The Alpha costs $900, the Omega is $1,400, and the Summit retails for $1,900. SkyRock does not sell their up-scale bicycles through typical retail channels but instead operates on a mail-order and phone-in basis, taking only credit cards as payment. The company advertises extensively in bicycle magazines. They are currently shipping 2,000 bicycles a day, with a three- to four-week delivery delay between the time a customer places an order and the actual delivery of a bicycle.

SkyRock's bicycles are all produced on a make-to-order basis. Each frame is custom built according to the physical characteristics of the customer. The customer measures the length of his or her inseam, arms, and torso and enters these specifications on order forms that accompany SkyRock's magazine advertisements. The order form is then faxed, phoned, or mailed to SkyRock's headquarters in Big Rock, Arkansas. Orders are entered into the company's database as soon as they are received. The ITEM relational table (see Figure 4.10) is used by the operations scheduling department to develop and update the master production schedule for the assembly line and the materials planning department; in essence, each instance of the ITEM relational table *is* used to make the master production schedule. The

continued on next page

---

[1] Some of the ideas for this case were adapted from an article by Susan Moffat, "Japan's New Personalized Production," *Fortune*, October 1990, pp. 132–135. The article discusses The National Bicycle Industrial Company's flexible manufacturing process in Kokubu, Japan.

assembly line has three stages: frame construction, painting, and final assembly. Materials used in the construction of the bicycles are requisitioned from within SkyRock or are obtained from external suppliers. SkyRock has entered into long-term contracts with suppliers for many components, including tires, rims, and derailleurs.

SkyRock constructs their own frames in-house. Each bike has a unique bar code identifier that is assigned when the bike is ordered. The bar code is tied to the vertical post component of the frame as soon as the frame enters the production process. It is possible to determine where a bike is in the production process because the bar code is scanned when it enters a production stage. At the end of each day, a bike status report is prepared detailing which and how many bikes have passed through a particular stage in the assembly line. This information is also used to update the customer order file, which means customers can call SkyRock and find out exactly where their bike is in the production process at any given moment.

Figure 4.10 presents a high-level entity relationship diagram for the SkyRock case, which is described in Highlight 4.1. The SkyRock example does not reflect all the very complex applications and application databases found in modern manufacturing firms, but it does reflect some of the newer concepts in production operations management and provides a good starting point for constructing an ER diagram for a manufacturing environment. The relational tables for the ER diagram follow:

CUSTOMER	(<u>CID</u>, ADDRESS, PHONE, FAX#, PAYMENT_METHOD)
ORDER	(<u>ORDER_ID</u>, *CID*, ORDER_DATE, TOTAL_COST, EXPECTED_SHIPPING_DATE, ACTUAL-DATE-SHIPPED)
ITEM	(<u>BAR_CODE_ID</u>, *ORDER_ID, BIKE_MODEL, PRODUCTION_STAGE*, ERGONOMIC_SPECS, MISCELLANEOUS_SPECS)
PROCESS	(<u>PRODUCTION_STAGE</u>, STAGE_DESCRIPTION, STAGE_LOCATION)
BIKE	(<u>BIKE_MODEL</u>, BIKE_DESCRIPTION, BIKE_COST)
HAS-BOM	(*<u>BIKE_MODEL</u>, <u>PART_ID</u>*, QUANTITY)
PART	(<u>PART_ID</u>, PART_DESCRIPTION)
PART-SUPPLIER	(*<u>PART_ID</u>, <u>SID</u>*)
SUPPLIER	(<u>SID</u>, TYPE_OF_SUPPLIER {*external or internal*})

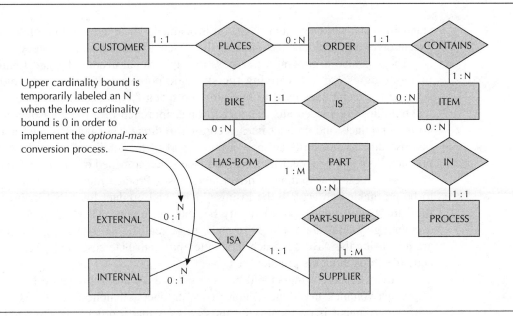

Upper cardinality bound is temporarily labeled an N when the lower cardinality bound is 0 in order to implement the *optional-max* conversion process.

FIGURE 4.10 High-Level Entity Relationship for SkyRock Inc.

INTERNAL   (DEPARTMENT_NAME, *SID*, BUILDING,
                  PHONE_NUMBER)

EXTERNAL   (SUPPLIER_NAME, *SID*, SUPPLIER_ADDRESS,
                  SUPPLIER_PHONE)

ACTIVITY-BASED COSTING

Another important topic influencing the design of production operations management databases is activity-based costing (ABC). The ABC approach is such an important topic in production operations management and management accounting that we present some background material before discussing the ER diagram.

There is an emphasis in management accounting on linking accounting to strategy through the development of what are called strategic cost analysis systems.[2] In strategic cost analysis, the process of measuring and evaluating costs is done in the context of the corporate goals and objectives. The entire process is driven by a multistage cycle involving formulating strategy, communicating the strategy throughout the organization, developing a plan to implement the strategy, and establishing controls to monitor activities. Establishing controls (budgets,

[2] Shank, John K., and Govindarajan, Vijay, *Strategic Cost Analysis: The Evolution from Managerial to Strategic Accounting*, R.D. Irwin, Homewood, Illinois, 1989.

standard costs, variances, and return on investment) is an attempt to monitor the execution of organizational activities as they relate to implementing strategy.

There is also a growing awareness that traditional accounting and finance methodologies are undermining the strategic potential of new technologies because the techniques used to measure and quantify the benefits of emerging technologies are inaccurate.[3] The traditional approach of allocating overhead costs to products and product lines according to direct labor hours is misleading because direct labor costs are now a minor part of the total cost of producing a product. Poor strategic decisions can be made when so-called overhead and fixed costs are allocated according to direct labor costs. Product lines that are thought to be profitable can actually be losing money, and product lines that look as if they are losing money can in reality be making money when traditional cost accounting systems are in place. To make more realistic decisions, organizations are now using the ABC approach in an attempt to attribute costs and revenues to activities throughout the product life cycle.

Activity-based costing should be used when there are significant differences in product volumes and in the complexity of product assemblies. The focus in an ABC environment is on identifying the *activities* that a product is subjected to during its life cycle. Each product is thus assigned to activities involving product design, product engineering, machine setups, product processing, parts delivery, quality control, marketing, and distribution.

The primary advantage of the ABC approach is that it improves the traceability of overhead costs, thereby providing management with more accurate unit cost data to use in assessing the viability of product lines, the benefits of automation technologies, and the effectiveness of new process technologies.

The increased accuracy of ABC systems is accompanied by an increase in measurement costs for two reasons. First, activity-based systems have more cost drivers than volume-based cost systems.[4] Second, ABC systems are most accurate when they measure resource consumption in real time. To reduce the cost of measurement, some of these systems use indirect measures of resource consumption, such as the number of orders processed, the number of shipments processed, and the number of inspections performed.

Measuring transaction volume is in effect a surrogate measure for the rate at which resources are being consumed. Advanced technologies such as bar code readers, optical character readers, automated parts identification, and computer-aided process monitoring can be used to measure the duration of an activity in real time and the amount of resources consumed by that activity. The results include more accurate and more unobtrusive measures of resource consumption.

[3] Noori, H. *Managing the Dynamics of New Technology*, Prentice Hall, Englewood Cliffs, New Jersey, 1990.

[4] Cooper, R., and Kaplan, R. S., *The Design of Cost Management Systems*, Prentice Hall, Englewood Cliffs, New Jersey, 1991.

Figure 4.11 illustrates an ER diagram that could be used to capture resource consumption in real time for a given process. The total activity time for a product is captured in the PRODUCED-BY table. You will notice by examining the relational tables for this diagram that since an employee and a machine do not have to be involved with the product for the total duration of the activity, they also have starting and ending times. To find what products an employee works on would require a relational *join* involving the EMPLOYEE, EMP-ACT, ACTIVITY, PRODUCED-BY, and PRODUCT tables.

The ER diagram in Figure 4.11 presents a potential solution to the complex problem of tracking product cost drivers. The relational tables for the ER diagram follow:

PRODUCT	(<u>PID</u>, PRODUCT_DESCRIPTION)
PRODUCED-BY	(*<u>PID</u>, <u>AID</u>*, START_TIME, END_TIME)
ACTIVITY	(<u>AID</u>, ACTIVITY_DESCRIPTION)
EMP-ACT	(*<u>AID</u>, <u>EID</u>*, EMPLOYEE_START_TIME, EMPLOYEE_END_TIME)

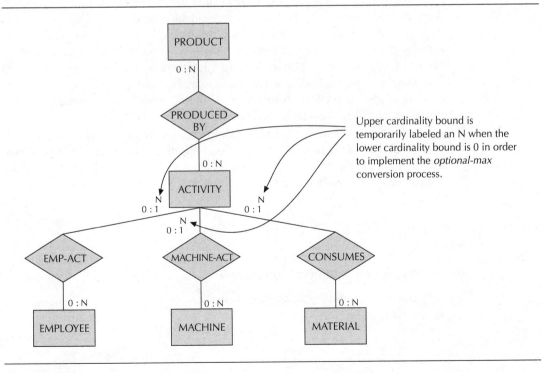

FIGURE 4.11   Activity-Based Costing

EMPLOYEE	(<u>EID</u>, EMPLOYEE_NAME)
MACHINE-ACT	(<u>*AID*</u>, <u>*MID*</u>, MACHINE_START_TIME, MACHINE_END_TIME)
MACHINE	(<u>MID</u>, MACHINE DESCRIPTION)
CONSUMES	(<u>*AID*</u>, <u>*MATERIAL_ID*</u>, #_OF_UNITS_USED)
MATERIAL	(<u>MATERIAL_ID</u>, MATERIAL_DESCRIPTION {*includes materials, parts, and utilities*})

Note the presence of the three intersection tables, EMP-ACT, MACHINE-ACT, and CONSUMES. These tables are the result of applying the *optional-max* rule to the business rules that are represented on the ER diagram.

SUMMARY

The ER diagram is an effective way to represent knowledge about various organizational subsystems. In this chapter, we presented a catalog of the types of knowledge you can use as a starting point for the ER modeling process. We presented applications in human resources, technical and maintenance support, reservations, charities, and production operations management. The ER modeling language is very straightforward; however, designing databases with an ER diagram requires knowledge of business and business applications along with an understanding of the art of ER modeling. This catalog of ER diagrams coupled with input from database books and periodicals that discuss database design can help you initiate the data modeling process. Knowledge of the business comes with experience, education, and close interaction with users.

In the next chapter, we outline an approach for constructing an enterprisewide data model. The enterprisewide data model is an ER diagram that captures broad-based knowledge about the organizational data resource at a very high level of abstraction that can be used to address the strategic application of database technology.

Review Questions

1. Develop an ER model for one of the application areas discussed in this chapter for a particular organization.

2. Can you identify entities that appear or can be found across many organizations?

Strategic Database Planning Using a Generic Data Model[1]

5

Key Concepts

value chain concept
enterprisewide generic data model
organizational complexity
information intensity

[1] This chapter is based on "Strategic Database Planning" in *Database Programming & Design*. Copyright *Database Programming & Design*, November 1990, Vol. 3, No. 11. Used with permission of Miller Freeman Publications Inc.

Now that we have discussed the basics of ER modeling and have looked at some examples of several industry-specific ER applications, let's turn our attention to the broader issues of strategic planning and strategic database planning. In this chapter, we introduce the concept of the enterprisewide generic data model as it relates to organizational strategic planning and strategic database planning. First, we briefly discuss the current state of information systems planning. Then we focus on generic data models in this context. Finally, we outline the phases for developing a strategic database plan using the enterprisewide generic data model.

THE CURRENT STATE OF INFORMATION SYSTEMS PLANNING

The current state of information technology can best be summarized by looking at the organizations in which this technology resides. Organizations often emphasize short-run returns rather than long-term benefits, and hence fail to integrate key business subsystems, making information retrieval from data repositories difficult. This lack of planning for using existing information has resulted in ineffectual decision-making and an alarming scarcity of long-term organizational vision and direction.

Some forward-thinking organizations are solving these problems with information systems designed to create a competitive advantage, such as large integrated database systems and network hardware and software. On-line reservation systems, order entry systems, and customer support systems use wide-band transmission lines, high-performance hardware, and sophisticated interface technologies to communicate with these databases.

From a managerial perspective, these systems have been successful. They have resulted in greater operational efficiency and the development of unique or differentiated products and services, the two primary competitive strategies an organization can employ. The success of these so-called competitive databases has prompted management to begin instituting a formalized approach to identifying emerging technologies with competitive potential. The process is normally executed in the corporate planning process or, in some organizations, in the information systems planning process.

Unfortunately, there are several problems with this process. First, strategic planning approaches need to be abstract and very conceptual because they deal with superordinate organizational goals. As a result, most of the current corporate planning approaches and information systems planning approaches are difficult to apply and implement because they do a poor job of modeling meta-level or macro-level organizational entities.

For instance, Porter and Millar[2] cite the **value chain concept** as an example of an approach an organization can use to exploit information to realize competitive

[2] Porter, C. E., and Millar, V. E., "How Information Gives You Competitive Advantage," *Harvard Business Review*, Vol. 63, No. 4, July–August 1985, pp. 149–160.

opportunities. Value chain analysis looks toward the five major organizational activities—inbound logistics, operations, outbound logistics, marketing and sales, and customer service—to improve competitiveness (see Figure 5.1). In reality, however, the value chain concept is difficult to implement because it is so highly abstract.

		Supplier Value	Firm Value	Distribution Value	Channel Value	After Market Value
Support Activities	Firm Infrastructure	Planning models				
	Human Resource Management	Automated personnel scheduling				
	Technology Development	Computer-aided design		Electronic market research		
	Procurement	On-line procurement of parts				
		Automated warehouse	Flexible manufacturing	Automated order processing	Telemarketing Remote terminals for salespersons	Remote servicing of equipment Computer scheduling and routing of repair trucks
		Inbound Logistics	Operations	Outbound Logistics	Marketing and Sales	Service

Primary Activities

Activity	Definition
Inbound logistics	Materials receiving, storing, and distribution to manufacturing premises.
Operations	Transforming inputs into finished products.
Outbound logistics	Storing and distributing products.
Marketing and sales	Promotion and sales force.
Service	Service to maintain or enhance product value.
Corporate infrastructure	Support of entire value chain, such as general management, planning, finance, accounting, legal services, government affairs, and quality management.
Human resource management	Recruiting, hiring, training, and development.
Technology development	Improving product and manufacturing process.
Procurement	Function or purchasing input.

FIGURE 5.1   Information Technology Value Chain[*]

[*]Adapted from Cash, J. I., McFarlan, F. W., McKenney, J. L., and Vitale, M. R., *Corporate Information Systems Management*, Irwin, 1988, p. 129. Original source: Porter, M. E., and Millar, V. E., "How Information Gives You Competitive Advantage," *Harvard Business Review*, July–August 1985, p. 151.

There are two fundamental difficulties with information systems planning as it is currently applied. The first problem is how to align information systems planning with the strategic planning process. The second problem is that both information systems planning approaches and strategic planning processes are weak in providing starting points or direction. In particular, they do not provide insight into identifying where information technology can be applied. Strategic database planning (SDP) using the enterprisewide generic model alleviates these problems by providing a focal point and by assisting in identifying technological opportunities for solving problems and improving competitiveness.

ENTERPRISEWIDE GENERIC DATA MODELING

During the strategic database planning, an **enterprisewide generic data model**, also called a macro-level data model, is developed to describe data requirements at a very high level. This model, which can be thought of as a template or blueprint for organizational databases, can be developed using either a top-down or bottom-up approach. In the top-down strategy, a limited number of high-level entities (in some instances, only one entity) are identified. Senior-level managers are employed to delineate the macro-level entities and then decompose them into more detailed entities and relationships using some form of top-down refinement. Output reports that have been targeted to senior-level managers are also examined to identify the macro-level entities.

Top-down enterprisewide data modeling can continue to any level of detail. As the decomposition process proceeds toward the operational activities of the firm, managers, supervisors, knowledge workers, and clerical personnel are all solicited to assist in constructing what are referred to as micro-level views of the enterprisewide data model. Operational and transaction data, such as input forms, reports, record formats, and input and output screens, are also examined to identify entities and determine database requirements. The data models in Chapter 4 are very close to being micro-level data models.

In the bottom-up approach, the process is just the opposite. It begins at the operational level of the business and ends at the top. First, the organizational data is examined to identify entities and determine database requirements. Then, managers, supervisors, knowledge workers, and clerical personnel are employed to provide input and validate these micro-level data models. Finally, input from senior-level managers is sought to complete the enterprisewide data model.

In practice, organizations use a combination of the top-down and bottom-up strategies because, independent of the other, each approach has its problems. In the bottom-up approach, for instance, input from senior-level managers is delayed until the enterprisewide data modeling process is nearly complete. This goes against the grain of well-known tenets that managerial support and user participation are necessary for implementing a comprehensive process such as enterprisewide data modeling. Senior-level managers are, after all, the most important stakeholders of organizational databases and strategic information systems.

The top-down approach has two major problems. First, operational input can be delayed too long, and input from individuals who participate in the day-to-day activities of the business may never get incorporated into the enterprisewide data model. Of course, an easy solution to this problem is to have early involvement in the modeling process by individuals from the operational level. The second problem with the top-down approach is that there is no starting point for initiating the enterprisewide data modeling process, no place to begin the decomposition process. The strategic database planning approach using generic data provides that missing starting point and alleviates many of the problems associated with both the top-down and bottom-up approaches.

GENERIC DATA MODELS AND STRATEGIC DATABASE PLANNING

Inmon[3] points out that generic data models conserve resources because organizations do not have to reinvent the wheel. Instead, organizations can use generic data models to increase the precision and availability of knowledge about the enterprise and to assist in uncovering areas of omission and commission. Additionally, as Scheer and Hars[4] point out, macro-level data models can assist in communicating and integrating the different business views of departments.

Although Inmon sees little strategic advantage to be gained by borrowing generic models from other companies because the data is at a too high level of abstraction, I believe there is a meta-level generic data model that organizations can use to identify technological opportunity points in the strategic planning process. This generic data model is at the highest level of abstraction and is basically the systemic model of the firm.

[3] Inmon, W. H., "The Jump Start to a Real Payoff," *Database Programming Design*, Vol. 1, No. 8, August 1988, pp. 21–24.

[4] Scheer, A-W, and Hars, S., "Extending Data Modeling to Cover the Whole Enterprise," *Communications of the ACM*, Vol. 35, No. 9, September 1992, pp. 166–172.

The generic data model (shown in Figure 5.2) consists of eight meta-level, macro-level, or superclass entities: customers, orders, products/services, processes, human resources, machines, raw materials, and suppliers.

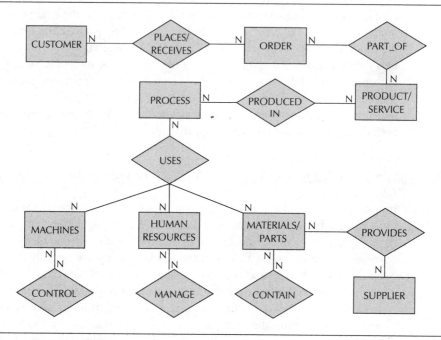

FIGURE 5.2   Generic Organizational Data Model

In the context of strategic database planning, the generic data model can help answer two fundamental questions: what business should the firm be in, and how will it conduct that business? The first question defines the essence of the business and is answered at the corporate level by stockholders, top-level management, the board of directors, and various other constituencies who have a stake in the organization. The answer to the second question is somewhat stable in the short run and can be answered in terms of transportation, manufacturing, service, communications, and so on. Over the long term, however, the answer to both questions may evolve with changes in the competitive environment and, in particular, with advancements in the capabilities of information technology. For example, airlines are certainly in the transportation business, but they have also evolved into tourism and reservation processing services. It is essential, therefore, that the corporate planning process provides a mechanism for discerning where to apply emerging information technologies. Once again, strategic database planning provides such a focus through the use of generic data models.

This section outlines the phases of the SDP process. The SDP process is not necessarily as linear as it appears here. In practice, there is a degree of concurrency in the SDP phases because technological availability, technological sophistication, and changes in the competitive environment are inextricably linked with the planning process.

Phase I: Determine Current Strategic Position

The primary activity in this first phase is understanding the organizational system and its business. Here it is necessary to identify the products and services the company produces, generate customer profiles, understand the factors of production (people, raw materials, machines), identify sources of materials, and develop an overview of the input–output transformation process (see Figure 5.3). In addition, historical and cultural background information should be gathered to develop a better understanding of firm direction. A high-level data flow diagram or context data flow diagram that illustrates the flow of data and objects between the high-level entities is a useful accompaniment in understanding system dynamics and components.

1. **Current Management Profile**

   Current organizational goals and objectives
   Values
   Personal goals
   Commitment and emphasis
   Skills
   Style

2. **Products and Services**

   Description of products and services produced

3. **Description of Production Process**

   Batch or continuous process
   Labor intensity
   Raw materials
   Machinery

4. **Resource Profile**

   Current capital position
   Availability of capital
   Facility characteristics: age, location, repair, sophistication

   Human resource characteristics: age, skill, education, and availability
   Raw material shrinkage and storage
   Sophistication of machinery

5. **Market Profile**

   Characteristics of customers
   Market dynamics, supply and demand
   Company and product image
   Market share
   Market penetration
   Product life cycle

6. **Characteristics of Suppliers**

   Number of suppliers
   Availability of materials
   Relationship with competitors

7. **Miscellaneous Environmental Profile**

   Government regulatory agencies
   IRS
   Political/social

FIGURE 5.3   Basic Structural Considerations for Strategy Formulation

Phase II: Determine Organizational Direction

The basic structural factors of the firm gathered in phase I are now used to answer long-range planning and policy questions related to customers, products, suppliers, distribution, promotion, competitive emphasis, pricing, and credit decisions. The primary questions to be asked are as follows:[5]

- **Customer policy**: What customer or customer segments are sought? What degree of granularity is needed for identifying customer segments? What type and level of customer service will be provided?

- **Product and process policy**: What products and product lines will be offered? How and when will products be made? Will product production be out-sourced?

- **Distribution and promotion policy**: By what mechanism, how quickly, and when will products and services be distributed to customers? What strategies and outlets will be used to promote the products and services?

- **Supplier policy**: How, from whom, and when will materials be ordered? What types of contractual relationships will be maintained with suppliers? How will material quality be monitored?

- **Competitive emphasis policy**: How can unique firm advantages (dealer, product quality, pricing, special services, and so forth) be exploited? Do the other strategic variables support this emphasis?

- **Pricing and credit policy**: What pricing and credit structure should be selected? How do firm image and industry characteristics influence the pricing and credit policy?

- **Financing policy**: What is an acceptable debt ratio? How will new sources of capital be acquired? What type of dividend policy will the company pursue?

- **Investment policy**: How and on what criteria will resources be allocated to projects, receivables, inventory, manufacturing, product development, human resources, overseas expansion, and so forth?

These questions are used to prompt the development of the enterprisewide data model and the ensuing strategic database requirements. The initial construction of the macro-level data model is an ambitious undertaking, but it is, nevertheless, the most critical phase in strategic database design. At this point, the generic data model (see Figure 5.2) can be used to identify strategic databases.

---

[5] Adapted from R. L. Katz, *Management of the Total Enterprise*, Prentice Hall, Englewood Cliffs, New Jersey, 1970.

Phase III: Use the Generic Data Model to Identify the Cardinality Between the Meta-Level Entities

Identifying the cardinality between products, processes, and resources provides useful insight into the workings of the organization. I have temporarily labeled the cardinality between all meta-level entities as N:N. The cardinality (1:1, 1:N, N:M) between the meta-level entities in the generic data model serves two functions. First, from a design standpoint, it assists in identifying the necessity of intersection tables and foreign keys. Note, though, that macro-level cardinality is not a critical consideration with a generic data model because these models are very abstract and very far removed from the details of implementation. More important, macro-level cardinality is an indicator of **organizational complexity**. Organizations with numerous many-to-many macro-level relationships between the meta-level entities are complex. This complexity is not necessarily a problem but can be exploited since there are more opportunities to redesign databases and apply advanced technologies.

Cardinality is, in fact, a good way to assess what Porter and Millar refer to as **information intensity**. Companies with large numbers of suppliers and customers, companies with numerous products and parts, and companies with a large number of steps in the manufacturing process are, according to Porter and Millar, information intensive. Industries that are information intensive tend to use information technology as competitive weapons. The degree of cardinality across the generic data model is a rough approximation of the level of information intensiveness.

Phase IV: Use the Generic Macro-Level Data Model to Identify Potential Database Opportunity and Technology Points to Exploit

The structural characteristics of the firm determined in phase I, the organizational policy decisions discussed in phase II, and the cardinality relationships delineated in phase III are now combined to identify potential competitive strategies. The focus is on developing database and technological solutions related to increasing input and output efficiency, differentiating products from competitors, and improving the organization's competitive position (see Figure 5.4). Potential questions to be answered include:

- What customer information can and should be obtained, and how can information technology be employed to support the gathering and maintenance of customer information?

- Can new information technology products and services be developed for different customer segments?

1. **Improving Environmental Control by**

   Better understanding of customers and market dynamics.
   Building barriers to market entry.
   Altering intraindustry competitive balance.
   Altering balance of power between firm and suppliers.

2. **Differentiating Products by**

   Delivering unique products.
   Delivering customized products.
   Delivering higher-quality products.

3. **Increasing Input/Output Efficiency by**

   Being the low cost producer.
   Reducing inventory levels, lead times, and investment in accounts receivables.
   Effective utilization of machines and human resources.

FIGURE 5.4   Potential Competitive Strategies*

*Adapted from Davis, G. B., and Olson, M. H., *Management Information Systems: Conceptual Foundations, Structure and Development*, McGraw-Hill, New York, 1985.

- What information is necessary to support order entry, and how can information technology be employed to support the order entry process?

- What information is necessary to support customer service, and how can information technology be employed to support customer service?

- What kind of information should be gathered to improve the production process, and how can information technology be employed to support the production process?

- What product quality indicators should the firm monitor, and how can information technology be employed to support quality control?

- What information is necessary to support human resources deployment and maintenance, and how can information technology be employed to support human resources?

- How should factors of production be scheduled, and how can information technology be employed to support production scheduling?

- How should machine maintenance be monitored and controlled, and how can information technology be employed to support machine maintenance?

- How should the firm order from suppliers, how should vendor quality be monitored, and how can technology be employed to support supplier information systems?

Martin et al.[6] have developed a detailed list of questions that can be used to identify opportunities for applying information technology strategically. The questions, which are presented in Figure 5.5, can be used in conjunction with the generic data model to exploit information technology.

Questions Related to Suppliers

1. Can we use IT to gain leverage over our suppliers?
   Improve our bargaining power?
   Reduce their bargaining power?

2. Can we use IT to reduce purchasing costs?
   Reduce our order processing costs?
   Reduce supplier's billing costs?

3. Can we use IT to identify alternative supply sources?
   Locate substitute products?
   Identify lower-price suppliers?

4. Can we use IT to improve the quality of products and services we receive from our suppliers?
   Reduce order lead times?
   Monitor quality?
   Leverage supplier service data for better service to our customers?

5. Can we use IT to give us access to vital information in our suppliers that will help us reduce our costs?
   Select the most appropriate products?
   Negotiate price breaks?
   Monitor work progress and readjust our schedules?
   Assess quality control?

6. Can we use IT to give our suppliers information important to them that will in turn yield cost, quality, or service reliability advantage to us?
   Conduct electronic exchange of data to reduce their costs?
   Provide master production schedule changes?

Questions Related to Customers

1. Can we use IT to reduce our customer's cost of doing business with us?
   Reduce paperwork for ordering or paying?
   Provide status information more rapidly?
   By reducing our costs and prices?

2. Can we provide some unique information to our customers that will make them buy our products and services?
   Billing or account status data?
   Options to switch to more higher-value substitutes?
   By being first with an easy-to-duplicate feature that will simply provide value by being first?

[6] Martin, E. W., DeHayes, D. W., Hoffer, J. A., and Perkins, W. C., *Managing Information Technology: What Managers Need to Know*, 2d edition, Macmillan, New York, 1994, p. 514.

---

3. Can we use IT to increase a customer's costs of switching to a new supplier?
By providing proprietary hardware or software?
By making them dependent upon us for their data?
By making our customer service more personalized?

4. Can we use external database sources to learn more about our customers and discover possible market riches?
By relating buying behavior from us to buying other products?
By analyzing customer interactions and questions to us to develop customized products and services or methods of responding to customer needs?

5. Can we use IT to help our customers increase their revenues?
By providing proprietary market data to them?
By supporting their access to their markets through our channels?

Questions Related to Competitors

1. Can we use IT to raise the entry barriers of competitors into our markets?
By redefining product features around IT components?
By providing customer services through IT?

2. Can we use IT to differentiate our products and services?
By highlighting existing differentiators?
By providing new differentiators?

3. Can we use IT to make a preemptive move over our competition?
By offering something new because we have proprietary data?

4. Can we use IT to provide substitutes?
By simulating other products?
By enhancing our existing products?

5. Can we use IT to match an existing competitor's offerings?
Are competitor products and services based on unique IT capabilities or technologies and capabilities generally available?

FIGURE 5.5 Questions for Identifying Strategic Applications of Information Technology (IT)*

*Adapted from Martin, E. W., DeHayes, D. W., Hoffer, J. A., and Perkins, W. C., *Managing Information Technology: What Managers Need to Know*, 2d edition, Macmillan, New York, 1994, p. 514.

Phase V: Develop an Enterprisewide Data Model or a Subset Data Model of the Technological Opportunity Points

The macro-level data model itself is not used directly to generate the database schema because it is very abstract. Instead, more detailed micro-level data models are needed for defining the database description. Further refinement and detail can be added to the macro-level generic data model using the methods described in earlier chapters.

If the objective is total integration or a complex detailed assessment, then entities and relationships are exploded and attributes are added, and a complete data architecture is developed. Participation in the development of an enterprisewide data model should be broad based, involving managerial and staff personnel from the operational level of the firm who will work with or derive benefit from the database.

Since there is some danger that the enterprisewide data model will not be used because of the long lead times between its construction and ensuing applications, it is necessary that the 80/20 maxim and six-month rule be adhered to.[7] These tenets state that 80 percent of the benefit of data modeling will be realized with 20 percent of the effort and that the data modeling process should take no more than six months. The strategic data planning process requires a significant expenditure of organizational resources. This time and effort are often viewed as excessive by top management, particularly when they are unclear about the purpose of a strategic data model. It is therefore necessary to construct the enterprisewide data model as quickly as possible.

SUMMARY

Technology is indeed a multifaceted concept involving both hardware and software, but, most important, it reflects ideas. The generic data model can be used to identify data requirements, and it can also be used to understand where new ideas can be applied. The generic data model is a powerful tool that can be aligned with other planning approaches to identify technological opportunity points.

Strategic database planning should precede the implementation of major technological improvements to an organization's information architecture. It should, in fact, be the focal point of systems reengineering because it is one of the most implementation-independent strategies that can be adopted. Too often technologies such as electronic data interchange, distributed databases, object-oriented programming and design, point-of-sale systems, and just-in-time can take on a life of their own; they *become* the organizational strategy. In fact, they are not necessarily the strategy; rather, they are opportunities for facilitating the organizational strategy.

An important emphasis in strategic planning is integration of the various organizational functions. Integration and compatibility are dominant themes in a top-down approach to database design. A useful feature of SDP is that it adds structure to the conceptual activity of the strategic planning process. What's more, it provides a platform for communication and further elaboration of the enterprisewide data model throughout the various organizational levels. One of the key benefits of SDP is that it forces senior-level managers to look toward operations for strategic opportunities. As we noted earlier, this is precisely the area where many of the

---

[7] Adapted from Goodhue, D. L., Quillard, J. A, and Rockart, J. F., "Managing the Data Resource: A Contingency Perspective," *MIS Quarterly*, Vol. 12, No. 3, September 1989, pp. 373–392.

---

systems for competitive advantage have been applied. Because the SDP approach is based on data modeling, it provides a graphic illustration of where new technologies can be applied and how they will affect existing systems. The SDP process is an important methodology for the data administrator because it encourages the development of a strategic perspective toward the organization's information requirements. Sound strategic recommendations on the how, what, and where of applying information technology are scarce commodities. When these recommendations are related to the organizational mission rather than being solely focused on technology, they will be taken more seriously.

Review Questions

1. In your opinion, why have some organizations ignored the implementation of long-term information systems planning in favor of short-term solutions? What are some of the benefits of strategic planning and information systems planning? Conversely, what are some of their deficits?

2. Describe top-down and bottom-up data model development strategies. What are the advantages and disadvantages of each?

3. Describe the benefits of using the enterprisewide generic data model.

4. What are the five phases for developing a strategic data plan?

5. What role does cardinality between meta-level entities play in the generic model?

Object-Oriented Data Modeling

6

Key Concepts

objects
classes
object classification
methods
inheritance
polymorphism
replica models
symbolic models

In their purest form, philosophical and quality programming issues aside, systems written using object-oriented concepts present users with a better and more realistic model of the world than systems written with traditional languages using traditional systems analysis and design approaches. First, they are designed and implemented to look and act the way humans view systems. Second, systems written using object-oriented concepts and written in object-oriented programming languages have system components that can be reused. The notion of software reuse has been around for some time and has always been an important consideration of structured analysis, design, and programming, but with object-oriented programming languages and object-oriented concepts, it is much easier to implement software reusability.

As with any programming language, some sort of analysis and design is necessary in order to establish a firm conceptual foundation for the ensuing implementation. There are proponents of object-oriented development that insist that the terms *analysis* and *design* do not apply, because the phases of object-oriented development are blurred. However, if you look closely, most of the popular approaches to object-oriented development do have some form of analysis and design activity.

There are many incarnations of the object-oriented development process (OODP) and they are indeed blurred and iterative, but in general, the phases include:

object-oriented analysis (OOA)

object-oriented design (OOD)

object-oriented programming (OOP)

In this final chapter, we focus on the first phase, object-oriented analysis, paying particular attention to the concept of class modeling, which is very similar to entity relationship modeling. Before we present a detailed description of object-oriented development, let's introduce some definitions for the critical object-oriented concepts.

OBJECT-ORIENTED TERMS AND CONCEPTS

Objects and Classes

An **object** is a tangible or intangible thing that can be classified and uniquely identified. It is a real-world thing, such as a customer, the customer service department, the order processing department, a loan agreement, a managerial report, an order form, or an educational degree. Classification leads to the identification of attributes that are common to a **class** of **objects** and to the identification of methods that are also part of the class definition.

The focus in the object-oriented approach is to develop systems that are an analog of the real world. Thus, a system designed using an object-oriented perspective should take on a physical world perspective; in other words, it should look and act like the physical world. This is not to say that nonobject-oriented approaches do not adopt a similar perspective. Object-oriented developers, however, make a conscious effort to provide a high degree of symmetry between the object system and the reality of the users' environment.

One of the most important and, as it turns out, most difficult activities in object-oriented development is **object classification**—that is, determining how objects in the real world can be classified into some type of meaningful representation of knowledge. The concepts discussed in Chapter 2 can be readily applied to classifying objects because the semantic model is the conceptual foundation for object modeling, just as it is for ER modeling.

Classification

Recall from Chapter 2 that three semantic primitives are used to represent knowledge. Although these structural primitives were originally defined in Chapter 2 as classification schemes for knowledge, they can also be applied to classifying objects. The definitions are now slightly recast to reflect object-oriented terminology:

1. A class of objects can be constructed, described and qualified by the objects' attributes and by other classes (the *Is-part-of* structure). A class, then, is constructed from components consisting of attributes and other classes. This is referred to as the class *aggregation abstraction*.

2. A class can be related to other classes through subclasses (the *Isa* structure). Thus a subclass can inherit attributes from a superclass, and it can have its own unique attributes. This is referred to as the class *generalization and specialization abstraction*.

3. A class can interact with other classes, and a class can affect the attribute values of other classes through associations or collaborations (the *Is-associated-with* structure). This is referred to as the class *association abstraction*.

These three semantic structures are the foundation for understanding how classes relate to one another. They are used in some form or another by most of the popular object-oriented analysis and design approaches [for example, Rumbaugh et al., 1991; Short and Dodd, 1993; and Booch, 1994].

Aggregation and Association

In object-oriented data modeling, aggregation—the *Is-part-of* structure—and association—the *Is-associated-with* structure—are very similar classification mechanisms. Consider a situation where a customer fills out an order for a particular product. The ORDER class can be thought of as an aggregation of the CUSTOMER class and the ITEM class, where CUSTOMER *Is-part-of* ORDER and ITEM *Is-part-of* ORDER. The relationship between the ORDER class and the CUSTOMER class can also be viewed as an association, involving interaction and collaboration between the two classes, as illustrated in Figure 6.1. The association structure is used in instances where the relationship between classes can be described as some type of action. In Figure 6.1, the action is the placing of an order by the customer, where *placing* is modeled as an *Is-associated-with*.

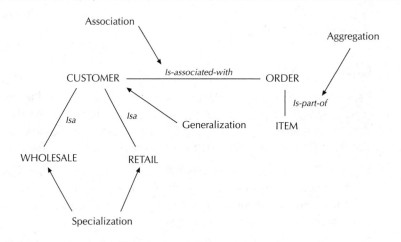

FIGURE 6.1   Semantic Primitives Classify Objects

The *Is-associated-with* structure is used to model relationships where classes participate in an activity that causes attribute values to change. Although the *Is-associated-with* relationship does not represent dynamic activity, per se, it does provide evidence that objects have engaged in transactions with other objects and that attribute values have been modified. Whenever there is a hint of dynamic activity between classes, it is preferable to use the *Is-associated-with* structure. More specifically, when a verb is used to describe the relationship between two classes, the relationship should probably be modeled as an association with the *Is-associated-with* structure.

As Rumbaugh et al. [1991] suggest, however, you should not spend too much time worrying whether aggregation or association should be used. Just pick the representation structure that makes sense and move on because aggregation and association can be implemented in an object-oriented programming language or object-oriented database with essentially the same effect.

Generalization and Specialization

Generalization and specialization are implemented in object-oriented approaches using the *Isa* structure, just as they were in ER modeling. A subclass in object-oriented design is essentially an entity *subtype* that participates in an *Isa* relationship. In Figure 6.1, for example, customers could be either wholesale or retail customers. Thus WHOLESALE *Isa* CUSTOMER and RETAIL *Isa* CUSTOMER. The generalization class—or superclass—would be CUSTOMER, and the specialization subclasses would be RETAIL and WHOLESALE.

The identification of *Isa* subclasses is an important activity because in the object-oriented paradigm, subclasses inherit both attributes and methods. This ability of classes to inherit methods is a distinguishing feature of object-oriented modeling. **Methods** are the programs, algorithms, or operations that are part of class definitions. They are encapsulated—that is, part of—class definitions, and an object that is assigned to a class can use the methods of that class.

Class Inheritance in Generalization and Specialization

Inheritance is a critical feature as well as a primary goal of object-oriented development. The emphasis in object-oriented development is on identifying class and subclass system hierarchies in a system. The generalization and classification of objects encourages the reuse of programming code because, in object-oriented programming languages and object-oriented database systems, a subclass can inherit data structures and methods from higher classes. A superclass, just like an entity supertype, has generalizable attributes and methods. Subclasses are specializations of the superclass and inherit all the data structures and methods of the superclass.

To illustrate this point, consider that in a banking environment a LOAN might be classified as a superclass, with MORTGAGE and COMMERCIAL as its subclasses (MORTGAGE *Isa* LOAN and COMMERCIAL *Isa* LOAN). A method that is defined at the loan superclass level can be used by all the subclasses. For example, calculating the payment amount for a loan, whether the loan was a mortgage or a commercial loan, is a function of the loan amount, the interest rate, and the term of the loan. The mortgage loan and commercial loan share a common method for computing payments that utilizes the time-value of money mathematics. The determination of the interest rate for each loan subclass, however, might be different. For example, the home equity interest rate might be tied to the prime rate, whereas the commercial rate might be a function of the credit rating of the company applying for the loan, the size of the loan, and the prime rate. The method for determining the interest for the two kinds of loans is referred to as polymorphic because the type of loan determines the specific way in which the interest rate is calculated. **Polymorphism** permits a method to respond differently to an object, that is, to invoke a different behavior according to the object's class characteristics. In effect, the methods (programs or algorithms) react differently according to the object type. Well-designed classes take advantage of polymorphic behavior.

CLASS MODELING APPROACHES

Now let's look at some examples of how the data modeling concepts discussed throughout this book relate to the object-oriented data modeling. We illustrate three approaches to class modeling. They are the Object Modeling Technique (OMT) [Rumbaugh et al., 1991], the Information Engineering/Objects (IE/O) approach [Short and Dodd, 1993], and the Booch notation [Booch, 1994].

OMT

Rumbaugh's Object Modeling Technique uses the three semantic structures to classify objects in the same way they are used in the construction of the ER diagram. Notice in the simple example presented in Figure 6.2 that both methods and attributes are associated with the classes. For example, for the Company class, the hiring and firing methods are part of the class in addition to the name, address, phone number, and primary product attributes. Also note that Person is a generalization of both the Worker and Manager specialization classes. The Worker and Manager subclasses will inherit the general methods and attributes of the Person, but they could also have specialized methods and attributes defined within the context of the subclass.

IE/O

Short and Dodd [1993] recently discussed an enhancement to Texas Instruments' Information Engineering (IE) methodology, which they call IE/O. Because Texas Instruments' IE methodology has always emphasized the importance of the data model, it should not be surprising that the IE/O approach will focus on the development of object classes since they are so similar to entities. Figure 6.3 presents an object model that includes classes, class attributes, and operations (the IE/O terminology for methods). Notice that the Foreign Order subclass inherits the attributes of Order, as well as the operation (method) for taking an order; however, it also has a specialized operation for arranging customs clearance. As of this writing, the IE/O approach is still under development at Texas Instruments.

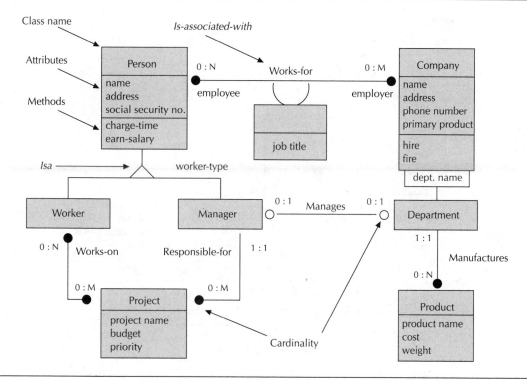

FIGURE 6.2   Object Model Technique*

*Adapted from Rumbaugh et al., 1991, p. 272.

Booch Notation

Figure 6.4 illustrates an example of a client–server system involving order processing using the Booch [1994] notation. The early focus in the Booch methodology is on identifying the classes. Attributes and methods are added only after the class definitions look stable. This strategy squares with Booch's [1994, p. 146] statement that "the identification of classes and objects is the hardest part of object-oriented analysis and design." Note that the original example did not contain any *Isa* structures, thus the Retail and Corporate specializations were added to the Customer class in this example. In addition, although Booch also has the facility to add methods to class definitions, this particular example did not include methods as part of the class definitions.

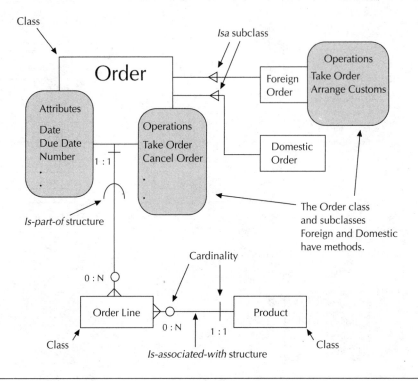

FIGURE 6.3   IE/O Notation[*]

[*]Adapted from Short and Dodd, 1993, p. 63.

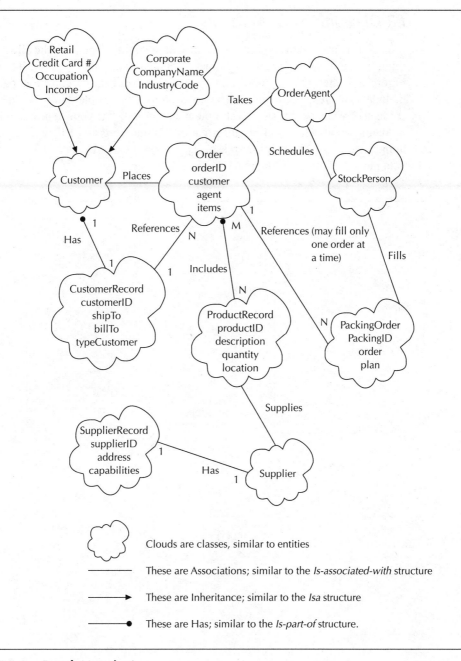

Clouds are classes, similar to entities

—————— These are Associations; similar to the *Is-associated-with* structure

————▶ These are Inheritance; similar to the *Isa* structure

————● These are Has; similar to the *Is-part-of* structure.

FIGURE 6.4   Booch Notation*

*Adapted from Booch, 1994.

ER Diagrams as OOA Models

Finally, it is important to point out that, with a slight adaptation, the ER diagramming notation can be adapted to object-oriented data modeling. As illustrated in Figure 6.5, the entity symbol and the relationship symbol can be expanded to include attributes and methods. The notation may be simple, but it works. As one student of object-oriented development has noted, "Anyone familiar with data modeling approaches such as Information Engineering and ER will feel right at home with OOA. The simple reason is that the heart of every OOA model is a data model" [Palmer, 1994, p. 61].

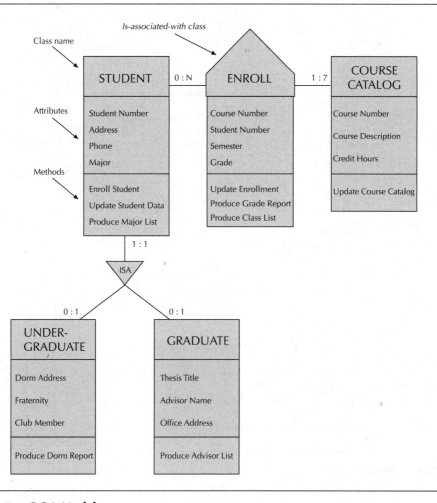

FIGURE 6.5   OOA Model

As we discussed in Chapter 1, the systems development process is actually an applied problem-solving process. Similarly, object-oriented development is also problem-solving, but it uses the object metaphor as a focal point for conceptualizing, modeling, and implementing a system.

There is still a systems development cycle in object-oriented development, including analysis, design, and implementation, but the focus here is on the structure of the classes and the behavioral interrelationships among classes. The process of identifying the objects and their associated object classes, and object instances and their methods, is very similar to contemporary development approaches in that it relies heavily on early prototyping and user participation during the development process.

Because there is an emphasis on actual coding in object-oriented development, there is disagreement in the information systems community on what activities are part of analysis, design, and implementation. As such, the process for conducting object-oriented design and the graphical tools for supporting OOD are in transition. Nonetheless, the phases and activities outlined here are typical of many object-oriented development approaches.

Object-Oriented Analysis Activities

- Identify relevant objects.
- Object-oriented data modeling: Classify objects according to their similarities and differences, and arrange them in class hierarchies. Develop an ER diagram-like static model of the classes. Identify the relevant attributes of each object, and post them to the appropriate class.
- Object-oriented process modeling: Identify the functional and dynamic behavior of objects. Construct data flow diagrams that illustrate the way in which objects transform data. Construct state transition diagrams that illustrate the various states an object can be in and how those states are affected by other objects.

Object-Oriented Design Activities

- Design user interface classes.
- Design file classes.
- Design detailed methods (algorithms, functions, or programs) for classes.
- Design the control structure for the object system. For example, the initial system startup, the menu structure, and the error handler.
- Detail the entire object package, that is, delineate software units in terms of the data structures and algorithms.
- Select OOP language and hardware.

Object-Oriented Programming Activities

■ Construct object software units.

■ Test and evaluate software units.

As we noted earlier, identifying objects and classifying objects in object-oriented analysis is the most critical part of object-oriented development. The generic data model described in Chapter 5 and the catalog of data models presented in Chapter 4 can be a useful starting point in building class libraries. They can also be used to initiate the development of a portfolio of generic enterprisewide object models for different industries.

For additional detail on all aspects of object-oriented analysis and design, particularly on modeling the dynamic behavior of classes and objects, see Rumbaugh et al. [1991] and Booch [1994].

OBJECT NORMALIZATION

Before concluding this chapter, we need to address the concept of object identity. There are two ways of storing instances in a class hierarchy in an object-oriented database [Kim, 1991]. The first approach is to require that an instance belong to one and only one class, and the second approach is to allow an instance to belong to more than one class. Be aware that significant system overhead is involved in updating object databases when the second approach is used because update anomalies can occur if the system does not deal effectively with the proliferation of object linkages.

For example, as the object-oriented database in Figure 6.6 illustrates, if an instance of Mr. Kim is deleted from the UNIVERSITY-PERSON object, then all the instances of Mr. Kim will also need to be deleted. If all the instances of Mr. Kim are not deleted, then the referential integrity of the database will be violated. Figure 6.7 presents an alternative design of the database, in which each instance can belong to one and only one class. This approach greatly reduces data redundancy and leads to a more stable database structure.

It should be apparent that from these examples that the concept of object normalization is also critical in designing object-oriented databases. This is a somewhat controversial issue. Many proponents of object-oriented languages argue that primary key fields are not needed to link objects because it is the responsibility of the object-oriented software to maintain transparent internal pointers that link related attributes and data structures.

Consider, however, that each object must have a unique identifier that is carried throughout its life. The object identity is in effect an identifier or primary key of sorts that can ensure data integrity and reduce redundancy. Unique objects need to be identified, and the attributes that are attached to an object instance should be functionally dependent on the object identity.

Be wary of any object-oriented approach that suggests that redundant copies of objects are acceptable. The concepts of normalization outlined in the Appendix are still applicable to the object-oriented paradigm, and they are essential to the long-term viability and integrity of all databases.

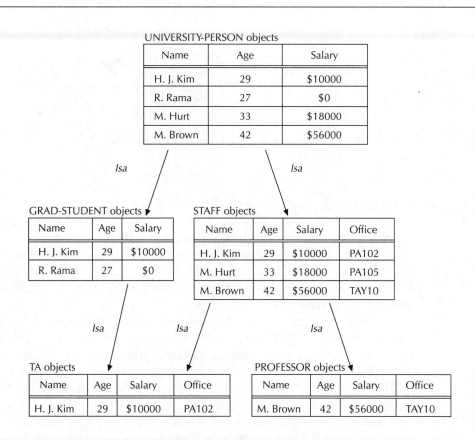

FIGURE 6.6   Object Instances Belonging to More Than One Class*

*Adapted from Kim, 1991, p. 29.

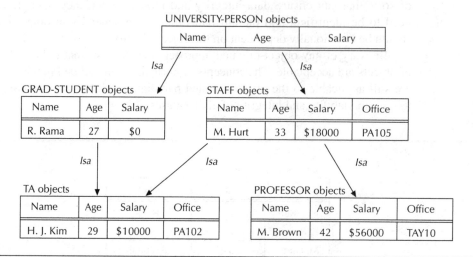

FIGURE 6.7   Object Instances Belonging to One and Only One Class*

*Adapted from Kim, 1991, p. 30.

EVALUATING MODELING APPROACHES

The object paradigm is indeed very powerful for modeling and implementing systems. It is, however, in a state of transition because both object-oriented languages and object-oriented database systems are maturing rapidly. Concomitantly, the development methodologies and graphical tools for object-oriented development are still under development.

Because there are so many new methodologies and tools for developing applications and so little research dedicated to understanding which tools facilitate the systems development process, most analysts rely on experience and rules of thumb [Cerveny, Garrity, and Sanders, 1990; Cerveny, Joseph, and Sanders 1992]. There is also much to be gleaned from the theory of models to help in evaluating tools and methods.

Chapanis [1961] suggests that all models should be judged on whether they provide for economy of description and whether they have the power to suggest implications that are not evident at first sight.

There are two basic types of models: **replica models** and **symbolic models**. Replica models look like the thing being modeled. For example, a globe is a replica model because it looks like the earth. A software prototype is a replica model because prototypes look or act like the system that is being constructed [Cerveny, Garrity, and Sanders, 1986]. In contrast, symbolic models rely on ideas, concepts, and symbols for representation. Graphical tools such as ER diagrams and object-oriented design diagrams fit the category of symbolic models.

There is a famous saying attributed to William of Ockaham [1285–1349?] known as Ockaham's razor. It states, "What can be done with fewer is done in vain with more." In other words, analysts should seek modeling tools that facilitate problem structuring and support communication, and be wary of tools that are merely fashionable. A modeling tool should be simple yet possess sufficient power to capture what is necessary to translate the specification into a computer application.

SUMMARY

In this chapter, we outlined the conceptual foundations of object-oriented modeling. We showed the semantic structural primitives—*Is-part-of*, *Isa*, and *Is-associated-with*—to be the foundation for class modeling. We discussed several different approaches to class modeling in terms of how they represent the structural primitives. We also presented general development approach for object-oriented systems and discussed the concept of object identity in the context of reducing redundancy and maintaining system integrity. In the final topic, which considered the role of tools in modeling systems, we suggested that the simplest tool that gets the job done is the best tool.

As we noted throughout this book, data modeling is a very powerful tool for simplifying the representation and conceptualization that facilitates the systems integration process. A commitment to integration requires long-term commitment to consistent product and process improvement if a truly viable, adaptive organization is to emerge. Object-oriented technology is a useful addition to the analyst's toolkit that assists in dealing with complexity and improving the process and product of systems development.

Review Questions

1. Why is object-oriented programming considered a more realistic model of the world?

2. How do the definitions and uses of the three semantic structures differ when they are used in object-oriented programming (versus ER modeling)?

3. What is inheritance? What is polymorphic inheritance? Why are these concepts so important in object-oriented programming?

4. Outline the phases and activities typically associated with object-oriented development approaches.

5. If you were evaluating modeling approaches, what criteria would you use?

Appendix:
Relational Table Normalization[1]

Key Concepts

normalization
deletion anomaly
update anomaly
insertion anomaly
functional dependency
transitive dependency
multivalued dependency
first normal form (1NF)
second normal form (2NF)
third normal form (3NF)
fourth normal form (4NF)
domain-key normal form (DKNF)

[1] Edgar F. Codd, the inventor of normalization, had this to say about the genesis of normalization: "We all have trouble organizing even our personal information. Businesses have those problems in spades. It seemed to me essential that some discipline be introduced into database design. I called it normalization because then-President Nixon was talking a lot about normalizing relations with China. I figured that if he could normalize relations, so could I." [Matthew H. Rapaport, "A 'Fireside' Chat," DBMS, Vol. 6, No. 13, 1993, pp. 54–60.]

Some analysts do not use ER diagrams in the conceptual phase of database design. Instead, they analyze existing file structures, look at input and output screens, collect input documents and output reports, and engage in frequent interviews with users on their information requirements. The information from these sources is then synthesized to identify relevant attributes and used to define the relational database tables. The formal approach for assigning the attributes to relational tables is called **normalization** [cf. Codd, 1972, and Codd, 1970].

When you use a conceptual design tool, like ER diagrams, you also perform this type of information analysis; however, the initial focus is on identifying entities, then assigning attributes to them. This is a top-down approach to database design. In the normalization approach, which is a bottom-up strategy, you do just the opposite: First you identify the attributes, and then you assign them to the relational tables—which, in substance, represent entities. In practice, skilled database designers draw on both processes when they are designing and reengineering databases.

Highlight A.1   *Identifiers or Primary Keys*[2]

The focus of the database design process revolves around identifying and assigning attributes to tables. Within this process, it is the identification of the primary key that establishes the foundation for database stability, integrity, and useability. The relational data model characteristics, along with the material on normalization presented in this Highlight, provide the necessary framework for developing guidelines for constructing and selecting primary key identifiers.

Guideline 1

The domain of the primary key should be large enough to accommodate the identification of unique rows for the next 100 years.

At first, having the ability to uniquely identify records for the next 100 years appears to be overzealous, but by thinking so far ahead, you will not have to worry about retiring old or inactive records in order to make room for additions.

Guideline 2

Primary keys should be a unique random collection of alphabetic, numeric, or alphanumeric characters.

The requirement that each row in a relational database has a unique primary key is often violated. Names are a particular problem when they are used as a primary key. Although the customer name is very useful for database navigation, there is always a chance that someone else will have the same key field. Just a few of the problems that can occur when keys are not

continued on next page

[2] For an in-depth discussion of this topic, see Whitener, T., "Primary Identifiers: The Basics of Database Stability," *Database Programming & Design*, Vol. 2, No. 2, January 1989, pp. 42–49.

unique include delivering merchandise to the wrong address, merchandise being shipped to multiple locations, and incorrect updating of an account. Many of these problems can be alleviated when organizations use unique random account numbers to identify customers. The primary keys are generated, tracked, and maintained with the assistance of computer software.

In some rare cases, uniqueness can be improved by adding another attribute to the customer's last name. For example, the customer's address or a phone number is added to the customer name to create a unique primary key. In general, however, names are best used only as database navigation attributes.

Guideline 3

Avoid using smart keys. Primary keys should not contain "fact giving" data. If these facts are necessary, they should be entity attributes.

Providing information in primary keys may introduce integrity problems over the long run. This type of primary key is attractive because it provides users with easily accessible attribute information; however, because the primary key contains attribute information, they may become difficult to update and keep current.

Smart keys are often found in inventory management and plant operations. Consider the following primary key value for a product:

VHSKOR0622

This refers to a type of videocassette recorder (VHS), made in Korea (KOR), with a model number of 0622. If the same product is subsequently manufactured in Taiwan, this key is meaningless. The country in which the product is manufactured and its type should become product attributes rather than primary keys. The information in smart keys can of course be part of the relational table definition and used in database navigation. The smart key can be used by users of the database as though it were a primary key.

In some organizations, the primary key has bill-of-materials information. For example:

FWHEEL-SPOKE4892

This means that spoke type 4892 is part of the front wheel. Again, the bill-of-materials structure should be developed using attributes (see the section "Recursive Relationships" in Chapter 2 to see how this is handled).

Guideline 4

Use the suffix ID in constructing primary keys (CUST_ID or CID, VENDOR_ID or VID, and so on).

It is very desirable to use the table name and the suffix ID as primary keys because the primary key is the cornerstone for maintaining, manipulating, and retrieving data from relational tables. Experience has shown that being able to quickly identify primary keys saves time and promotes communication.

Assigning attributes to the proper relational table can be a very tricky process, which is an artform that benefits from experience. When normalization is executed properly, however, it facilitates data integration, reduces data redundancy, and provides a robust architecture for retrieving and maintaining data. In this appendix, we discuss why normalization is important and how the various normal forms can be used to design databases. First, we discuss how poorly designed databases lead to data anomalies.[3]

DATA ANOMALIES

Deletion Anomalies

A **deletion anomaly** occurs when the removal of a record results in a loss of important information about an entity. For example, suppose all the information about a customer is contained in an ORDER file. If the customer calls up and cancels an order, customer information could also be lost when the order is deleted.

The description in Highlight A.2 of Recycled Tractor illustrates the way in which a deletion anomaly can cause problems. Recycled Tractor maintains leads on potential tractor acquisitions in the LEAD file. Suppose an individual who wants to sell a tractor to Recycled decides not to sell the tractor. If the policy of the company is to delete individuals from the LEAD file when they no longer have a tractor for sale, all the lead data (potential marketing information) would be lost from the current production database. Of course, the company could still retain relevant customer data in the LEAD file, but this would result in numerous null fields and would create data retrieval and update problems. Simply creating two files—one for holding tractor data and one for holding lead data—would solve many database design problems for Recycled Tractor.

[3] Identifiers—or primary keys—play an important part in the normalization process. Highlight A.1 provides several guidelines to help you select indentifiers or primary key attributes.

Highlight A.2 Recycled Tractor

Recycled Tractor buys used and damaged tractors, refurbishes them, and then resells them. Recycled Tractor obtains the tractors from repair shops, auctions, farmers who simply want to sell their old tractors, and a variety of other sources in the agricultural industry. The individuals who search for the used tractors are called trackers. When a lead on a potential tractor is obtained, the tracker calls up the individual who wants to sell the tractor and asks him or her questions about the tractor manufacturer, the tractor model, and the year the tractor

continued on next page

was built. Sometimes a lead has tractors at more than one location. For example, a farmer might own two or three other farms and have a tractor for sale at each location.

Two individuals, called evaluators, are assigned to examine each tractor on site. An evaluator goes to the address of the tractor, appraises its value, and then calls in a bid on the tractor. After both bids have been received, the tracker makes a judgment on the value of the tractor, then contacts the lead and makes an offer to the owner of the tractor. If the tracker and the lead can agree on the price, the tracker purchases the tractor.

Recycled Tractor currently maintains all this information in one computer file called the LEAD file, which contains 2,000 records. Approximately 1,500 of the records in the LEAD file involve 1 or 2 tractors, and the remaining 500 records have between 3 and 20 tractors associated with a lead. The layout of the LEAD file is presented next.

LEAD (LEAD_ID, LEAD_NAME, LEAD_ADDRESS, LEAD_BANK, LEAD_PHONE#, TRACKER_NAME, TRACKER_PHONE#, TRACTOR1_ID, MANUFACTURER1, MODEL_NAME1, YEAR_BUILT1, TRACTOR_ADDRESS1, ASKING_PRICE1, AMOUNT_PAID1, EVAL1_TRAC1_NAME, EVAL1_TRAC1_CELL#, EVAL1_TRAC1_BID, EVAL2_TRAC1_NAME, EVAL2_TRAC1_CELL#, EVAL2_TRAC1_BID, ..., TRACTOR20_ID, MANUFACTURER20, MODEL_NAME20, YEAR_BUILT20, TRACTOR_ADDRESS20, ASKING_PRICE20, AMOUNT_PAID20, EVAL1_TRAC20_NAME, EVAL1_TRAC20_CELL#, EVAL1_TRAC20_BID, EVAL2_TRAC20_NAME, EVAL2_TRAC20_CELL#, EVAL2_TRAC20_BID)

LEAD file: Primary key = LEAD_ID. The data items have been indented to illustrate repeating groups.

Fields	Description
LEAD_ID	The unique identifier for each individual selling a tractor
LEAD_NAME	The name of the individual selling the tractor or tractors to Recycled Tractor
LEAD_ADDRESS	The address of the individual selling the tractor
LEAD_BANK	The name of the lead's bank
LEAD_PHONE#	The lead's phone number
TRACKER_NAME	The name of the employee who searches for tractors
TRACKER_PHONE#	The tracker's phone number
TRACTOR1_ID	The tractor identifier for the first tractor
MANUFACTURER1	The description for the first tractor

MODEL_NAME1	The model name for the first tractor
YEAR_BUILT1	The year the first tractor was built
TRACTOR_ADDRESS1	The address for the first tractor
ASKING_PRICE1	The amount the lead wants for the first tractor
AMOUNT_PAID1	The amount paid for the first tractor
EVAL1_TRAC1_NAME	The name of the first evaluator who evaluated the first tractor
EVAL1_TRAC1_CELL#	The first evaluator's cellular phone number
EVAL1_TRAC1_BID	The amount the first evaluator bid for the first tractor
EVAL2_TRAC1_NAME	The name of the second evaluator who evaluated the first tractor
EVAL2_TRAC1_CELL#	The second evaluator's cellular phone number
EVAL2_TRAC1_BID	The amount the second evaluator bid for the first tractor

⋮

TRACTOR20_ID	The tractor identifier for the 20th tractor
MANUFACTURER20	The description for the 20th tractor
MODEL_NAME20	The model name for the 20th tractor
YEAR_BUILT20	The year the 20th tractor was built
TRACTOR_ADDRESS20	The address for the 20th tractor
ASKING_PRICE20	The amount the lead wants for the 20th tractor
AMOUNT_PAID20	The amount paid for the 20th tractor
EVAL1_TRAC20_NAME	The name of the first evaluator who evaluated the 20th tractor
EVAL1_TRAC20_CELL#	The first evaluator's cellular phone number
EVAL1_TRAC20_BID	The amount the first evaluator bid for the 20th tractor
EVAL2_TRAC20_NAME	The name of the second evaluator who evaluated the 20th tractor
EVAL2_TRAC20_CELL#	The second evaluator's cellular phone number
EVAL2_TRAC20_BID	The amount the second evaluator bid for the 20th tractor

Update Anomalies

An **update anomaly** occurs when multiple record changes for a single attribute are necessary when a change to only one record in the database should be necessary. For example, suppose that one of the tractor evaluators at Recycled Tractor obtained a new cellular phone number. In that case, every record in the LEAD file (2,000 records) would have to be searched, and the cellular phone number for that particular tractor evaluator would have to be changed. The same update anomaly would exist if one of the trackers' phone numbers changed, too.

Insertion Anomalies

An **insertion anomaly** occurs when there does not appear to be any reasonable place to assign attributes and attribute values to records in the database. There are two types of insertion anomalies: (1) adding new attributes to a record and (2) updating only part of a record.

In the first type, an attempt is made to add a data field to a record, but the record does not seem to be the right place to put the field. In the case of Recycled Tractor, management might decide to capture additional information on each evaluator in order to keep track of his or her whereabouts. Suppose, for instance, that the evaluator's home address and phone number were added to the LEAD file. Adding these attributes would generate a great deal of redundant data in the database because the information would be repeated over and over in every LEAD record to which the evaluator was assigned. There is another problem that is more subtle but in some ways more difficult to solve; it is the essence of the insertion problem.

A decision has to be made on when to enter values into the database for a new employee who will be an evaluator. Should Recycled Tractor immediately assign the evaluator to the first available lead? What if the lead is in training for several months? Until an evaluator is assigned to the database, there is no information on the evaluator in the LEAD file. There is another strategy. A new record could be *inserted* in the LEAD for the evaluator. The record would have values for the evaluator's name, cellular number, home address, and home phone number. The rest of the record, including the primary key LEAD_ID, would, of course, contain null values. Only part of the record would be updated.

Adding additional attributes to the LEAD file for evaluators or the trackers is a major problem. The file is already riddled with null values. Consider that Recycled Tractor purchases only one or two tractors from the majority of the 2,000 records in the LEAD file. But each of these records has room for data on 20 tractors.

Many organizations have "superfiles" like Recycled Tractor's LEAD file. Indeed, they may even be having a modicum of success with such a structure. Notwithstanding the obvious storage inefficiencies of such a file structure, the real problem with this configuration is in database navigation because it becomes increasingly cumbersome to retrieve and maintain 1:N and N:M data relationships. Alone, none of the insertion, deletion, and update anomalies would cause insurmountable problems. Competent application developers could generate the appropriate reports and maintain the integrity of the database. As the business evolves and product lines broaden, as customers demand more sophisticated services, and as transaction volumes increase, however, the database begins to deteriorate.

ELIMINATING MODIFICATION ANOMALIES USING NORMALIZATION

Normalization facilitates the elimination of addition, deletion, and insertion anomalies. When the mechanics of normalization are first observed, it appears to be a very complex process. This is understandable because there are almost as many ways to interpret and define normalization as there are textbooks on database design. For many students of database design, the normalization process is much simpler when it is coupled with ER modeling because the ER approach promotes the development of functionally dependent attributes. In fact, it is not unusual to find the files and tables are already in third normal form after constructing an ER diagram. One basic rule, with two corollaries, underlies the normalization process. The basic rule is:

> The attribute values in a relational table should be functionally dependent on the primary key value.

Its corollaries are:

1. No repeating groups are allowed in relational tables.
2. A relational table cannot have attributes involved in a transitive dependency with the primary key.

When the basic rule and its corollaries are executed on relational tables, the relational tables enter a particular normal form. We discuss the five normal forms shortly.

First, remember from our earlier discussions in the chapters on data modeling that it is the organization that determines what data is important and how the different entities and attributes are related. Although the analyst is sometimes an advocate of a certain design, more often than not, he or she is the observer and facilitator for discovering the organizational data semantics. One of the primary responsibilities of the database designer is to formalize data relationships by identifying the dependencies among the attributes. The different types of dependencies are critical to understanding and executing the normalization process. Several concepts and definitions related to data dependencies need to be articulated before the normal forms are presented.

Functional Dependency (FD)

A **functionally dependent** relationship exists between two attributes when one attribute value implies or determines the attribute value for the other attribute. There is the notion of causality between attribute values in this relationship because an attribute value is a direct determinant of another value. For example, the value for LEAD_NAME always determines the value for the LEAD_BANK. In a more formal notation, LEAD_NAME —> LEAD_BANK, which translates to the LEAD_NAME attribute value functionally determining the LEAD_BANK attribute value. Thus, the name of the lead is a determinant of the bank name. Conversely, LEAD_BANK value does not functionally determine the attribute value for the LEAD_NAME.

A functional dependency between two attributes can also be reciprocal, that is, in both directions. For example, assuming that each employee has a unique name, EM_SS_NUM —> EM_NAME and EM_NAME —> EM-SS_NUM. This can be written as:

EM_SS_NUM —> EM_NAME

EM_NAME —> EM_SS_NUM

This translates to the attribute value for EM_SS_NUM functionally determining the attribute value for EM_NAME, and the attribute value for EM_NAME functionally determining the attribute value for EM_SS_NUM. Thus the employee name is a determinant of the employee social security number, and the employee social security number is a determinant of the employee name. Attributes in which the functional dependencies are reciprocal are said to be totally dependent on one another.

Transitive Dependency

Transitive dependencies occur when a nonkey attribute value is functionally dependent on another nonkey attribute value that is not a candidate key. For example, suppose that for the following relational table HOURLY RATE is functionally dependent on JOB CATEGORY:

EMPLOYEE (EMPLOYEE_ID, JOB_CATEGORY, HOURLY_RATE)

If JOB_CATEGORY = SUPERVISOR

then the employee HOURLY_RATE is $15.00 per hour.

If JOB_CATEGORY = WELDER

then the employee HOURLY_RATE is $13.50 per hour.

Thus HOURLY_RATE is functionally dependent on the JOB CATEGORY, which is functionally dependent on EMPLOYEE_ID. In formal terms:

EMPLOYEE_ID —> JOB_CATEGORY

JOB_CATEGORY —> HOURLY_RATE.

The relational table as just defined can lead to update anomalies because of the way in which the attributes are related through functional dependencies. For instance, if the hourly rate for welders changes from $13.50 to $14.50 per hour, then all the welder records will have to be updated. To avoid this problem, a separate table should be created that contains the JOB_CATEGORY as the primary key and the HOURLY_RATE as an attribute. The presence of a separate table requires only the welder record to be updated when the hourly rate changes.

Transitive dependencies do not occur in the following situation:

A —> B

B —> A

B —> C

In this situation, B is a candidate key for the relational table, and this will not lead to modification anomalies.

When the middle attribute (B) is a candidate key, it could just as easily be used as the primary key. For example, suppose that in the preceding scenario only one employee filled a given job category. This situation might occur when an organization has, say, 100 unique jobs, each of which is filled by one and only one employee. In essence, there would be a reciprocal, totally dependent relationship between EMPLOYEE_ID and JOB_CATEGORY; therefore, JOB_CATEGORY could be used as an identifier in the EMPLOYEE table.

If a relational table has been properly normalized, the primary key is always a determinant of the nonkey attributes in a table. In other words, the nonkey attributes are functionally dependent only on the primary key.

Multivalued Dependency (MVD)

Multivalued dependencies are the result of having multiple values for a particular attribute. There are three types of multivalued dependencies: *simple*, *independent*, and *transitive*. Most of our discussion is related to the simple multivalued dependencies.

A simple multivalued dependency between two attributes is similar to the 1:N cardinality relationship discussed in Chapter 2. For example, consider a 1:N relationship between a faculty member and the courses he or she is teaching during a particular semester. The COURSE_ID, which includes the course number and the section number, is a unique identifier for each course being taught in the semester.

In addition, each faculty member is uniquely identified by a FACULTY_ID. In this particular example, a faculty member is associated with a set of courses, but a course is associated with only one faculty member. This is represented as:

FACULTY_ID —>> COURSE_ID

COURSE_ID —> FACULTY_ID

These relationships translate to the value for FACULTY_ID functionally determining the values for the COURSE_ID, and the value for the COURSE_ID functionally determining the value for FACULTY_ID. The —>> symbol is used to represent the multivalued dependency.

Functional dependencies can be determined for all the attributes related to a faculty member and courses taught by a faculty member. Adding additional attributes would result in the following dependency diagram:

FACULTY_ID —> F_NAME

FACULTY_ID —> OFFICE#

FACULTY_ID —>> COURSE_ID

COURSE_ID —> C_NAME

COURSE_ID —> CREDITS

The multivalued N:M dependency between the student identifier and course identifier is represented as:

STUDENT_ID —>> COURSE_ID

COURSE_ID —>> STUDENT_ID

This translates to the value for STUDENT_ID functionally determining multiple values for the COURSE_ID, and the value for the COURSE_ID functionally determining multiple values for STUDENT_IDs.

In the Recycled Tractor example (see Highlight A.2), each tractor a farmer is willing to sell would be an example of a multivalued dependency between the lead identifier and the tractors. Thus LEAD_ID functionally determines the multiple values for the TRACTOR_ID, or in formal notation, LEAD_ID —>> TRACTOR_ID. Conversely the relationship from TRACTOR_ID to LEAD_ID is functionally dependent. The TRACTOR_ID functionally determines the attribute value for the LEAD_ID. The dependencies between the LEAD_ID and the TRACTOR_ID are: LEAD_ID —>> TRACTOR_ID and TRACTOR_ID —> LEAD_ID.

The other two types of multivalued dependencies, independent and transitive, involve three or more attributes. Usually these types of multivalued dependencies are automatically eliminated with ER modeling and the execution of the first three steps of relational table normalization.

In this section, we explain each of the five phases of the normalization process in the context of the Recycled Tractor example. As you will see, normalization leads to a more understandable and more streamlined database structure.

The attributes for the LEAD file are repeated here. Please refer to Highlight A.2 for a detailed description of the attributes.

LEAD   (LEAD_ID, LEAD_NAME, LEAD_ADDRESS, LEAD_BANK, LEAD_PHONE#, TRACKER_NAME, TRACKER_PHONE#, TRACTOR1_ID, MANUFACTURER1, MODEL_NAME1, YEAR_BUILT1, TRACTOR_ADDRESS1, ASKING_PRICE1, AMOUNT_PAID1, EVAL1_TRAC1_NAME, EVAL1_TRAC1_CELL#, EVAL1_TRAC1_BID, EVAL2_TRAC1_NAME, EVAL2_TRAC1_CELL#, EVAL2_TRAC1_BID, . . ., TRACTOR20_ID, MANUFACTURER20, MODEL_NAME20, YEAR_BUILT20, TRACTOR_ADDRESS20, ASKING_PRICE20, AMOUNT_PAID20, EVAL1_TRAC20_NAME, EVAL1_TRAC20_CELL#, EVAL1_TRAC20_BID, EVAL2_TRAC20_NAME, EVAL2_TRAC20_CELL#, EVAL2_TRAC20_BID)

First Normal Form (1NF)

A relational table or file is in **first normal form** (1NF) if no attributes form repeating groups. The repeating group attributes are removed by creating another table. For Recycled Tractor, this means the repeating group of attributes for the 1 to 20 tractors are removed by creating a new table—the TRACTOR table—which holds the repeating group attributes. A linkage is made between the original table and the new table by posting the identifier from the original table into the new table. In this case, the LEAD_ID is posted to the TRACTOR table.

There is also a repeating group for the two evaluators who are assigned to appraise the value of the tractor. A new table is created—the EVALUATOR table—which contains attributes on the evaluator and his or her bid on a tractor. A linkage is made between the TRACTOR table and the EVALUATOR table by posting the tractor identifier, TRACTOR_ID, as a foreign key to the EVALUATOR table.

Putting the LEAD file in first normal form results in the following relational tables:

LEAD   (<u>LEAD_ID</u>, LEAD_NAME, LEAD_ADDRESS, LEAD_BANK, LEAD_PHONE#, TRACKER_NAME, TRACKER_PHONE#)

TRACTOR	(TRACTOR_ID, *LEAD_ID*, MANUFACTURER, MODEL_NAME, YEAR_BUILT, TRACTOR_ADDRESS, ASKING_PRICE, AMOUNT_PAID)
EVALUATOR	(EVAL_NAME, *TRACTOR_ID*, EVAL_CELL#, EVAL_BID)

As we demonstrated in Chapter 2, 1:N cardinality is handled through foreign keys. The tractors in the TRACTOR table are thus linked to a LEAD by posting the primary key in the LEAD table as a foreign key in the TRACTOR table. With this structure, data redundancy is minimized because it will not matter how many tractors are for sale—1 or 100. Whatever the number, there will be only one record for each tractor, and, more important, there is only one record for each lead.

Second Normal Form (2NF)

A relational table or file is in **second normal form** (2NF) when all nonkey attributes are functionally dependent on the entire key. Second normal form is specifically targeted at tables in which the rows are identified by a concatenated primary key.

The EVALUATOR table is the only table that has a concatenated key after being converted to 1NF. Let's examine EVAL_BID and EVAL_CELL# in the EVALUATOR table to see if either of these attributes violates 2NF. Remember, only tables with concatenated primary keys will have a problem in meeting the 2NF requirement.

The evaluator's bid attribute (EVAL_BID) complies with 2NF requirement because the bid is functionally dependent on the concatenated key comprised of the evaluator's name (EVAL_NAME) and the tractor identifier (TRACTOR_ID). In formal notation, {EVAL_NAME, TRACTOR_ID} —> EVAL_BID. The entire key is needed to determine the evaluator's bid on a particular tractor.

The evaluator's cellular phone number (EVAL_CELL#), on the other hand, does not meet the 2NF requirement because its value is not functionally determined by the concatenated key comprised of the evaluator's identifier (EVAL_NAME) and the tractor identifier (TRACTOR_ID). Instead, the evaluator's cellular phone number is functionally determined only by the evaluator's name, that is, EVAL_NAME —> EVAL_CELL#. The dependency {EVAL_NAME, TRACTOR_ID} —> EVAL_CELL# is actually a partial dependency because only the evaluator's name is needed to identify the cellular phone number.

The way to rectify this problem, and convert the EVALUATOR table to 2NF, is to create an intersection table called BID. The TRACTOR table and the EVALUATOR tables would thus be linked by posting the tractor identifier (TRACTOR_ID) and the evaluator identifier (EVAL_NAME) to the new intersection table BID. The creation of the BID table puts the tables in second normal form. The new table (BID) also has semantic appeal because it has a narrow theme—evaluator tractor bids.

Placing the tables in second normal form would lead to the following relational tables:

LEAD	(<u>LEAD_ID</u>, LEAD_NAME, LEAD_ADDRESS, LEAD_BANK, LEAD_PHONE#, TRACKER_NAME, TRACKER_PHONE#)
TRACTOR	(<u>TRACTOR_ID</u>, *LEAD_ID*, MANUFACTURER, MODEL_NAME, YEAR_BUILT, TRACTOR_ADDRESS, ASKING_PRICE, AMOUNT_PAID)
BID	(*<u>TRACTOR_ID</u>*, *<u>EVAL_NAME</u>*, EVAL_BID)
EVALUATOR	(<u>EVAL_NAME</u>, EVAL_CELL#)

The evaluator's cellular phone number is now functionally dependent on the entire primary key, which in this case is the evaluator's name. Similarly, the evaluator's bid on a tractor is functionally dependent on the concatenated key comprised of the tractor identifier and the evaluator's name.

Another attractive feature of this table configuration is that it will be easy to add additional information to the database for each evaluator. In other words, the address and home phone attributes could be added to the EVALUATOR table without causing redundancy problems.

Organizations and database designers intuitively shy away from using concatenated keys as table identifiers for critical organizational entities. This is not to say that they do not exist. In fact, concatenated keys proliferate in intersection or associated tables, where concatenated primary keys are used to link many-to-many relationships. The use of ER modeling and the *optional-max* approach for converting the ER diagrams to relational tables makes it highly unlikely that attribute values will be posted to the wrong table and that 2NF will be violated.

Third Normal Form (3NF)

A relational table or file is in **third normal form** (3NF) when it is in second normal form and no transitive dependencies exist and all attribute determinants are also candidate keys.[4] The primary objective in placing tables in third normal form is to get rid of all types of transitive dependencies. Second normal form dealt with transitive dependencies involving the primary key. Third normal form now examines the remaining transitive dependencies, including transitive dependencies involving nonkey attributes.

[4] This is actually an alternative, more restrictive, definition of third normal form, referred to as Boyce-Codd normal form (see Elmasri and Navathe, 1994], that reduces the chance of introducing transitive dependency anomalies.

One example of a transitive dependency in the revised Recycled Tractor database violates third normal form: The TRACKER_PHONE# is functionally dependent on the TRACKER_NAME, which is, in turn, functionally dependent on the primary key LEAD_ID. In more formal terms:

LEAD_ID —> TRACKER_NAME

TRACKER_NAME —> TRACKER_PHONE#

The way to correct this problem is to create a new table and place the attributes involved in the transitive dependencies in the relational table. Putting the tables in third normal form results in the following relational structures:

LEAD	(LEAD_ID, *TRACKER_NAME*, LEAD_NAME, LEAD_ADDRESS, LEAD_BANK, LEAD_PHONE#)
TRACTOR	(TRACTOR_ID, *LEAD_ID*, MANUFACTURER, MODEL_NAME, YEAR_BUILT, TRACTOR_ADDRESS, ASKING_PRICE, AMOUNT_PAID)
BID	(*TRACTOR_ID, EVAL_NAME*, EVAL_BID)
EVALUATOR	(EVAL_NAME, EVAL_CELL#)
TRACKER	(TRACKER_NAME, TRACKER_PHONE#)

One new relation is created—the TRACKER table—to deal with the transitive dependency. The primary key for the TRACKER table, the TRACKER_NAME, is posted as a foreign key in the LEAD table. The TRACKER_PHONE# is now functionally dependent on the TRACKER_NAME for its value. This will create the proper linkage for database navigation.

The LEAD table has been fully normalized at this point. There are two additional phases of the normalization process, but we present them in abstract terms because converting tables to third normal form should be adequate for maintaining database integrity. Finally, an ER diagram presented in Figure A.1 could have been used to develop relational tables instead of the normalization process.

Fourth Normal Form (4NF)

A relational table or file is in **fourth normal form** (4NF) when all multivalued dependencies have been removed, including independent multivalued dependencies and transitive multivalued dependencies. No tables in the Recycled Tractor example have independent and transitive multivalued dependencies. In most situations, the process of putting tables in each of the first three normal forms removes these types of multivalued dependencies.

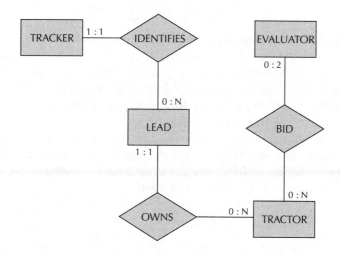

FIGURE A.1   ER Diagram for Recycled Tractor

Domain-Key Normal Form (DKNF)

A relational table or file is in **domain-key normal form (DKNF)** if every constraint on the table or file is the result of defining primary keys for a relational table and defining domains for the attributes in a relational table or file. Edit rules for attributes, the way attributes are related, and functional and multivalued dependencies are all examples of data constraints. In essence, the DKNF approach is a philosophy that focuses on developing themes for tables. For example, a STUDENT table contains attributes about students, and a FACULTY table contains attributes on the faculty theme. Because the DKNF approach attempts to decompose tables according to themes, it is very similar to the ER modeling approach (see Kronke [1992] for an overview of the DKNF approach). The *optional-max* approach, when coupled with ER diagrams, should result in the same relational schema as the DKNF approach.

The benefits of additional levels of normalization decrease rapidly after relational tables have been put into third normal form. The instances where higher-level normalization strategies are necessary are considered rare and theoretical. For a very in-depth discussion of the various normal forms, see Courtney and Paradice [1992] and Elmasri and Navathe [1994].

Normalization is an excellent supplemental tool that can provide an additional check on the stability and integrity of the ER diagram. The most important rule to keep in mind during the development of the ER diagram is that all attributes for an entity should be functionally dependent on the primary key. This simple meta-rule derived from the normal forms will provide the necessary foundation for data integration and database stability.

In practice, experienced systems analysts use a combination of the bottom-up strategy of normalization and the top-down strategy of ER modeling. Both approaches are an important part of the analyst's toolkit because they facilitate the development of stable integrated databases.

References

Apte, U., and Winniford, M., "Global Outsourcing of Information Systems Functions: Opportunities and Challenges. " In *Managing Information Technologies in a Global Society*, ed. Medhi Khosrowpour. Harrisburg, PA: Idea Group Publishing, 1991, pp. 58–59.

Bailin, S. C., "An Object-Oriented Requirements Specification Method." *Communications of the ACM*, vol. 32, no. 5 (May 1989), pp. 608–623.

Batini, C., Ceri, S., and Navathe, S. B., *Conceptual Database Design: An Entity-Relationship Approach*. Redwood City, CA: Benjamin-Cummings Publishing Co., 1992.

Booch, G., *Object-Oriented Analysis and Design with Applications*, 2d ed. Redwood City, CA: Benjamin-Cummings Publishing Co., 1994.

Bruce, T. A., *Designing Quality Databases with IDEF1X Information Models*. New York: Dorset House Publishing Co., 1992.

Cardenas, A., *Data Base Management Systems*, 2d ed. Needham Heights, MA: Allyn and Bacon, 1985.

Cerveny, R., Garrity, E., and Sanders, G. L., "A Problem Solving Perspective on Systems Development," *Journal of Management Information Systems*, vol. 6, no. 4 (Spring 1990).

Cerveny, R., Garrity, E., and Sanders, G. L., "The Application of Prototyping to Systems Development: A Rationale and Model." *Journal of Management Information Systems*, vol. 3, no. 2 (Fall 1986), pp. 50–62.

Cerveny, R. P., Joseph, D. A., and Sanders, G. L.,"The Effects of Structured Methodologies on System Enhancement Efforts," working paper, School of Management, State University of New York at Buffalo, 1992.

Cervany, R. P., Pegels, C. C., and Sanders, G. L., ed., *Strategic Information Systems for Strategic Manufacturing, Operations, Marketing, Sales, Financial and Human Resources Management*. Greenwich, CT: JAI Press, 1993.

Cerveny, R., and Sanders, G. L., "Implementation and Structural Variables." *Information and Management*, vol. 11, no. 4 (November 1986), pp. 191–198.

Chandrasekaran, B., Johnson, T. R., and Smith, J. W., "Task-Structure Analysis for Knowledge Modeling." *Communications of the ACM*, vol. 35, no. 9 (September 1992), pp. 124–137.

Chapanis, A., "Men, Machines, and Models." *American Psychologist,* vol.16 (1961), pp. 113–131.

Chen and Associates Inc., *ER-Designer Reference Manual*. Baton Rouge. LA: Copyright, 1986–1990.

Chen, P. P. S., "The Entity-Relationship Model: Towards a Unified View of Data." *ACM Transactions Database on Systems*, vol. 1, no.1 (1976).

Choobineh, J., Mannino, M. V., and Tseng, V. P., "A Form-Based Approach for Database Analysis and Design," *Communications of the ACM*, vol., no. 2 (February 1992), pp. 108–120.

Coad, P., "Object-Oriented Patterns." *Communications of the ACM*, vol. 35, no. 9, (September 1992), pp. 153–159.

Coad, P., and Yourdon, E., *Object-Oriented Design*. Englewood Cliffs, NJ: Prentice Hall, 1991.

Codd, E. F., "Further Normalization of the Database Relational Model." In *Data Base Systems: Courant Computer Science Symposia*, 6. Englewood Cliffs, NJ: Prentice Hall, 1972.

Codd, E. F., "A Relational Model for Large Shared Data Banks." *Communications of the ACM*, vol. 13, no. 6 (June 1970).

Codd, E. F., and Date, C. J., "Much Ado About Nothing." *Database Programming and Design*, vol. 6, no. 10 (October 1993), pp. 46–53.

Cohen, P. R., and Feigenbaum, E.A., *The Handbook of Artificial Intelligence*. Heuristech Press, William Kaufmann, Inc., 1982.

Colter, M. A., "A Comparative Examination of Systems Analysis Techniques." *MIS Quarterly* (March 1984), pp. 51–66.

Courtney, J., and Paradice, D., *Database Systems for Management*, 2d ed. Homewood, IL:, Richard D. Irwin, 1992.

Curtis, W., Kellner, M. I., and Over, J., "Process Modeling." *Communications of the ACM*, vol. 35, no. 9 (September 1992), pp. 75–90.

D. Appleton Company, Inc., *Integrated Information Support Systems—Information Modeling Manual—IDEF1X Extended,* ICAM Project, Priority 6201, Subcontract No. 013–078–846, U.S.A.F., Prime Contract No. F33615–80–C–5155, Air Force Wright Aeronautical Laboratories, U.S. Air Force Systems Command, Wright-Patterson Air Force Base, Ohio, 1985.

Date, C. J., *An Introduction to Database Systems*, 5th ed. Reading, MA: Addison-Wesley, 1990.

Davis, W., *System Analysis and Design: A Structured Approach*. Reading, MA: Addison-Wesley, 1983.

Dearden, John, "MIS Is a Mirage," *Harvard Business Review*. vol. 50., no. 1 (January–February, 1972), pp. 90–99.

Dittrich, K. R., Gotthard, W., and Lockemann, P. C., "Complex Entities for Engineering Applications." In *Research Foundations in Object-Oriented and Semantic Database Systems*, ed. A. F. Cardenas and D. McLeod. Englewood Cliffs, NJ: Prentice Hall, 1990, pp. 303–321.

Elmasri, R., and Navathe, S. B., *Fundamentals of Database Systems*, 2d ed. Redwood City, CA: Benjamin-Cummings Publishing Co., 1994.

Evans, J. R., and Lindsay, W. M., *The Management and Control of Quality*. St. Paul, MN: West Publishing Company, 1993.

Fagin, R., "Multivalued Dependencies and a New Form for Relational Databases." *ACM Transactions on Database Systems*, vol. 2, no. 3 (September 1977), pp. 262–278.

Flavin, M., *Fundamental Concepts of Information Modeling*. Englewood Cliffs, NJ: Yordan Press, Prentice Hall, 1981.

Gillenson, M. L., "The Duality of Database Structures and Design Techniques." *Communications of the ACM*, vol. 30, no. 12 (1987), pp. 1056–1065.

Gitlow, S. G., and Gitlow, S. J., *The Deming Guide to Quality and Competitive Position*. Englewood Cliffs, NJ: Prentice Hall, 1987.

Goldstein, R. C., and Storey, V. C., "Unravelling IS-A Structures." *Information Systems Research (ISR)*, vol. 3, no. 2 (June 1992), pp. 99–126.

Hammer, M., and McLeod, D., "Database Description with SDM: A Semantic Database Model." *ACM Transactions Database Systems*, vol. 19, no. 3 (September 1987).

Hammer, M., and McLeod, D., "Database Description with SDM: A Semantic Database Model." In *Research Foundations in Object-Oriented and Semantic Database Systems*, ed. A. F. Cardenas and D. McLeod. Englewood Cliffs, NJ: Prentice Hall, 1990, pp. 34–69.

Hansen, Gary W., and Hansen, James V., *Database Management and Design*. Englewood Cliffs, NJ: Prentice Hall, 1992.

Henderson-Sellers, B., and Edwards, J. M., "The Object-Oriented Systems Life Cycle." *Communications of the ACM*, vol. 33, no. 9 (September 1990), pp. 142–169.

Howe, D. R., *Data Analysis for Data Base Design*, 2d ed. New York: E. Arnold, 1989.

Hull, R., and King, R., "A Tutorial on Semantic Database Modeling." In *Research Foundations in Object-Oriented and Semantic Database Systems*, ed. A. F. Cardenas and D. McLeod. Englewood Cliffs, NJ: Prentice Hall, 1990, pp. 1–33.

Inmon, W. G., *Effective Database Design*. Englewood Cliffs, NJ: Prentice Hall, 1981.

Kim, Hyoung-Joo, "Algorithmic and Computational Aspects of OODB Schema." In *Object-Oriented Databases with Applications to CASE, Networks, and VLSI CAD*, ed. Rajiv Gupta and Ellis Horowitz. Englewood Cliffs, NJ: Prentice Hall, 1991, pp. 26–61.

Kim, Won, "Object-Oriented Databases: Definition and Research Directions." *IEEE Transactions on Knowledge and Data Engineering*, vol. 2, no. 3 (September 1990), pp. 327–341.

Kronke, D. M., *Database Processing*. New York: Macmillan, 1992.

Loomis, M. E. S., *The Database Book*. Greenwich, CT: Macmillan, 1987.

Martin, J., *Strategic Data-Planning Methodologies*. Englewood Cliffs, NJ: Prentice Hall, 1982.

Martin, J., and Finklestein, C. *Information Engineering*, vols. 1–2. London: Savant Institute, 1981.

McFadden, F. R., and Hoffer, J. A., *Data Base Management*. Redwood City, CA: Benjamin-Cummings Publishing Co., 1985.

McGovern, D., "Classical Logic: Nothing Compares 2U." *Database Programming and Design*, vol. 7, no. 1 (January 1994), pp. 54–61.

McLeod, Dennis, "A Perspective on Object-Oriented and Semantic Database Models and Systems." In *Object-Oriented Databases with Applications to CASE, Networks, and VLSI CAD*, ed. Rajiv Gupta and Ellis Horowitz. Englewood Cliffs, NJ: Prentice Hall, 1991, pp. 12–25.

Monarchi, D. E., and Puhr, G. I., "A Research Typology for Object-Oriented Analysis and Design." *Communications of the ACM*, vol. 35, no. 9 (September 1992), pp. 35–47.

Navathe, S. B., "Evolution of Data Modeling for Databases." *Communications of the ACM*, vol. 35, no. 9 (September 1992), pp. 112–123.

Nerson, J., "Applying Object-Oriented Analysis and Design." *Communications of the ACM*, vol. 35, no. 9 (September 1992), pp. 63–74.

Nijssen, G. M., *Conceptual Schema and Relational Data Base Design*. Englewood Cliffs, NJ: Prentice Hall, 1989.

Page-Jones, M., "Comparing Techniques by Means of Encapsulation and Connascence." *Communications of the ACM*, vol. 35, no. 9 (September 1992), pp. 147–152.

Palmer, J. "Object-Oriented Development Tools Trying for Prime Time." *Application Development Trends,* vol. 1, no. 1 (January 1994), pp. 60–67.

Peckham, J., and Maryanski, F., "Semantic Data Models." *ACM Computing Surveys*, vol. 20, no. 3 (September 1988), pp. 153–189.

Porter, C. E., and Millar, V. E., "How Information Gives You Competitive Advantage." *Harvard Business Review*, vol. 63, no. 4 (July–August 1985), pp. 149–160.

Pressman, R. S., *Software Engineering: A Practitioner's Approach*, 2d ed. New York: McGraw-Hill, 1987.

Quillian, R., "Semantic Memory." In *Semantic Information Processing*, ed. M. Minsky. Cambridge, MA: MIT Press,1968, pp. 216–270.

Rubin, K. S., and Goldberg, A., "Object Behavior Analysis." *Communications of the ACM*, vol. 35, no. 9 (September 1992), pp. 48–62.

Rumbaugh, J., Blaha, M., Premerlani, W., Eddy, F., and Lorensen, W., *Object-Oriented Modeling and Design*. Englewood Cliffs, NJ: Prentice Hall, 1991.

Sanders, G. L., and Courtney, J., "A Field Study of Organizational Factors Affecting DSS Success." *MIS Quarterly*, vol. 9, no. 1 (March 1985), pp. 77–93.

Schank R. C., with Childers, P. G., *The Cognitive Computer on Language, Learning, and Artificial Intelligence*. Reading, MA: Addison-Wesley, 1984.

Scheer, A. W., and Hars, Alexander, "Extending Data Modeling to Cover the Whole Enterprise." *Communications of the ACM*, vol. 35, no. 9 (September 1992), pp. 166–172.

Schmid, H. A., and Swenson, J. R., "On the Semantics of the Relational Data Model." Proceedings 1975 ACM-SIGMOD: *International Conference on the Management of Data*.

Schniederjans, M. J., *Topics in Just-In-Time Management*. Needham Heights, MA: Allyn and Bacon, 1993.

Short, K., and Dodd, X., "Information Engineering with Objects." *Object Magazine,* vol. 3, no. 4 (November–December 1993), pp. 61–64.

Storey, V. C., "Relational Database Design Based on the Entity-Relationship Model." *Data and Knowledge Engineering* (North Holland), vol. 7, no. 1 (November 1991), pp. 47–83.

Storey, V. C., "Understanding Semantic Relationships," forthcoming in the *Very Large Data Bases (VLDB) Journal*.

Storey, V. C., and Goldstein, R. C., "Knowledge-Based Approaches to Database Design." Forthcoming in *Management Information Systems Quarterly*.

Teorey, T., and Fry, J., *Design of Database Structures*. Englewood Cliffs, NJ: Prentice Hall, 1982.

Whitener, T., "Primary Identifiers: The Basics of Database Stability." *Database Programming and Design*, vol. 2, no. 2 (January 1989), pp. 42-49.

Whitten, J. L., Bentley, L. D., and Barlow, V. M., *Systems Analysis and Design Methods*, 2d ed. Homewood, IL: Richard D. Irwin, 1989.

Wiederhold, G., *Database Design for File Organizations*. New York: McGraw-Hill, 1987.

Yourdon, E., and Constantine, L. L., *Structured Design: Fundamentals of a Discipline of Computer Program and Systems*. Englewood Cliffs, NJ: Prentice Hall, 1979.

Zachman, J. A., "A Framework for Information Systems Architecture." *IBM Systems Journal*, vol. 26, no. 3 (1987), pp. 276–292.

Index